Forests and Development

This book is a fully up-to-date study of the major issues facing forest conservation and the forestry industry, and considers developments at local, national and global levels. Environmental and development topics relating to each level are discussed – for instance, the use of forest products in a rural poverty context, corruption and forest harvesting, and consumption as a political device.

Delacote employs a quantitative approach in order to analyse the plight of tropical forests in the developing world, and in doing so produces a range of interesting conclusions. This methodology fills a crucial research gap in existing studies of forests in a development context – increased use of theoretical tools to interpret real-life situations might be beneficial to the field. Therefore, the first objective of this book is to provide a sample of theoretical analysis concerning the forest–development nexus. The second objective is to supply empirical economists with new theoretical insights, in the hope that results can emerge with conclusive field testing and relevant policy recommendations.

Each chapter of the analysis has two main components: a description of the context and the application of economic tools to this context. A common feature of the different chapters is to describe stylized contexts that may be found in several regions of the developing world. The main objective is to balance the tradeoff between precise descriptions of the contexts in question and enough generality to enable broad application of the analysis. This book applies tools of general economic theory to problems related to forests in developing countries: portfolio diversification, tragedy of the commons, political economy, resource curse and war of attrition. The work should be of crucial interest to all scholars of environmental and development economics.

Philippe Delacote is a Researcher in Environmental Economics at the Laboratory of Forest Economics (INRA, Nancy, France).

Routledge Explorations in Environmental Economics
Edited by Nick Hanley
University of Stirling, UK

Forests and Development
Local, national and global issues

Philippe Delacote

LONDON AND NEW YORK

First published 2012 by Routledge

2 Park Square, Milton Park, Abingdon, Oxon OX14 4RN
711 Third Avenue, New York, NY 10017, USA

Routledge is an imprint of the Taylor & Francis Group, an informa business

First issued in paperback 2016

British Library Cataloguing in Publication Data
A catalogue record for this book is available from the British Library

Library of Congress Cataloging-in-Publication Data
Delacote, Philippe, 1978-
    Forests and development: local, national, and global issues / Philippe Delacote.
    p. cm.
    Includes bibliographical references and index.
    1. Forests and forestry–Economic aspects.
    2. Forest policy–Environmental aspects.
    3. Deforestation.
    I. Title.
SD393.D43 2012
577.3–dc23   2011048695

ISBN: 978-0-415-49815-9 (hbk)
ISBN: 978-1-138-22486-5 (pbk)

Typeset in Times New Roman
by Sunrise Setting Ltd, Torquay, UK

To Emma, Thomas and Laura

Contents

List of figures

List of tables

Foreword

I have been working on forest-related issues from the economic point of view for 8 years, during which I have met many people who have helped me to improve as a researcher and as a person. Among them I would like to thank my supervisors Rick van der Ploeg and Pascal Courty, who have done much to improve my work. I would also like to thank people I have met at conferences and seminars, among them Charles Palmer, Arild Angelsen, Greg Amacher, Jo Albers, Aart de Zeeuw, Timo Goeschl, Pierre-André Chiappori, Avinash Dixit, Jean-Louis Combes and Pascale Combes Motel.

Of course, I would like to acknowledge the great contribution of my colleagues and co-authors, without whom I would never have been able to write some of the chapters of this book and other papers: Olivier Damette, Claire Montagné, Lydie Ancelot, Lucie Bottega, Lisette Ibanez, Franck Lecocq, Sylvain Caurla, Serge Garcia, Alexandre Sauquet, Ahmed Barkaoui, Solenn Leplay and Sophie Thoyer.

Life is not only about work, and I would like to express my heartfelt thanks to my closest friends, for the (very important) non-working part of those years and the foundation of the FE: Pedro, Julien, Roland, Laurent, Nadia and Tatiana. Last but not least, thanks to my parents, grandparents, to Christine, Hugues, JB and Marie for their support and love over the years. Thanks to Amélie for these past years.

Part I

Overview

Introduction

The world forests and deforestation

Forests cover about 4 billion hectares worldwide, which represents 30.3 percent of total land area. Deforestation is defined by the Food and Agriculture Organization (FAO) as a radical removal of vegetation to less than 10 percent crown cover. This definition refers to a change in the land use and long-term removal of tree cover (Angelsen and Kaimowitz 1999). Annual loss of tropical forests was estimated at 15.4 million hectares in the 1980s (FAO 1992), and at 12.7 million hectares in the 1990s (FAO 1997). Net annual loss was estimated at 7.3 million hectares in the *GEO Year Book* of the United Nations Environment Programme (UNEP 2006: 75). Latin America and the Caribbean region, which has the largest proportion of forest area, experienced a decrease in the forest cover from 49.2 percent in 1990 to 45.8 percent in 2005. Africa also shows a continued net loss of forest area, with 21.4 percent in 2005, compared to 23.6 percent in 1990. Forest areas in Europe, North America, Asia and the Pacific region remained stable and even increased slightly during this period. Overall, deforestation is most severe in developing countries such as Argentina, Brazil, the Democratic Republic of Congo, Indonesia, Myanmar, Mexico, Nigeria and Sudan (Smouts 2002).

Forests provide many environmental services, both at local and global levels. Locally, forests provide important hydrological benefits, preventing soil erosion and flood hazard. Globally, forests sequester carbon, and are therefore important in limiting global climate change. For instance, it is estimated that deforestation accounts for up to 20 percent of global greenhouse gas emissions (www.fao.org). Moreover, tropical forests are the most valuable ecosystem in the world: between 50 and 90 percent of the earth's species live in tropical forests (World Commission on Environment and Development (WCED) 1987). Deforestation thus represents a major environmental concern, both locally and globally.

Forests are not only an environmental indicator, but also a harvestable resource, which can create wealth and local development. Considering the fact that deforestation and forest degradation are now mostly localized in tropical regions of the developing world, it is an essential to be able to cope with forest issues in the context of development economics. Forests are, for instance, a perfect illustration of the poverty–environment nexus, but are also affected by important and broader development issues, such as corruption, rent-seeking behaviors, economic and environmental management. More generally, development of the occidental world has come about at the expense of high rates of deforestation, related to changes in land use. A crucial question is then to imagine new ways of taking development forward which can moderate forest losses.

Overall, deforestation is at the frontier of development and the environment, as forests constitute both an environmental concern and a renewable resource. Deforestation and forest issues are therefore a very interesting and challenging research object, extremely relevant in terms of public policies.

This book has several important characteristics. First, in order to underline the multiple geographical dimensions of forest concerns, it considers the three scales of interactions described above: local, national and global. Second, the objective of the book is to build bridges between environmental and developmental treatments of forests issues. Consequently, it is a book not only on forest economics, but also on environment and development economics. The analysis is indeed quite distant from traditional forestry economics (which deals with optimal forest management, forest rotations, and so on) and is closer to development economics dealing with environmental issues. Therefore, I have chosen for each scale one particular topic that seems to be particularly relevant, both on the development and the environmental side: the use of forest products in a rural poverty context, corruption and forest harvesting, and consumption as a political device.

The aim of the methodology adopted is to fill a crucial research gap in the field of forests in a development context, which consists of a relative lack of theoretical tools to decrypt real-life situations. Indeed, quite a lot of empirical and case studies may be found on this compelling issue. However, the analysis would sometimes benefit from rigorous theoretical argument. The content of this book, then, is deliberately theoretical, with a twofold methodological aim. The first objective is to give a sample of theoretical analysis concerning the forest–development nexus. The second objective is to provide empirical economists with new theoretical insights, in the hope that results can emerge with conclusive field testing and relevant policy recommendations.

Each chapter of the analysis has two main components: a context description and an application of economic tools to this context. A common feature of the different chapters is indeed a description of stylized contexts that may be found in several regions of the developing world. The main challenge here is to find the balanced trade-off between precise descriptions of the contexts considered and enough generality to fit with many cases of application of the analysis. It is thus important here to build on several case studies describing those contexts, and to extract the main common features among them. Once the context has been described, traditional economic analysis can be used. This book thus applies tools of general economic theory to problems related to forests in developing countries: portfolio diversification, the tragedy of the commons, political economy, resource curse and war of attrition.

The remaining parts of this introduction describe the three scales described above and provide non-technical summaries of the different chapters.

Local: forests and people

Agricultural expansion appears to be the most important cause of deforestation. Indeed, the share of deforestation related to agricultural expansion has been estimated at at least 50 percent in the 1980s (Myers 1992) and at 70 percent in the 1990s (UNEP 2003). In Africa, which has the highest deforestation rates in the world, more than 50 percent of the deforested zones have been switched into small farms. Deforestation is therefore mostly unplanned and beyond the direct control of governments. It is therefore crucial to understand the links between people and forests.

Poverty and environmental degradation are often said to constitute a vicious circle (UNEP 2000). Poor people are dependent on the environment, and thus overuse it, which makes them even poorer. The Brundtland report (WCED 1987), the first to underline the importance of poverty in environmental degradation, was followed by the 1992 Rio conference. The implicit conclusion of this link is the win–win potential of helping poor countries to develop while at the same time protecting the environment. Concerning the deforestation process, this vicious circle analysis appears to be appropriate, given that poor households are the main agents of deforestation. In Africa, this link appears to be related to the low productivity and input use of smallholder agriculture, which leads to land degradation and agricultural expansion (Reardon *et al.* 1999).

More than 1.6 billion people depend to varying degrees on forests for their livelihood. About 60 million indigenous people are almost wholly dependent on forests. Some 350 million people who live within or adjacent to dense forests depend on them to a large extent for subsistence and income. In developing countries, about 1.2 billion people rely on agroforestry farming systems that help to sustain agricultural productivity and generate income. Worldwide, the forest industry provides employment for 60 million people. One billion people depend on drugs derived from forest plants for their medical needs (World Bank 2001). Disregarding the problem of defining precisely the concept of forest dependency (see Wollenberg and Ingles 1998), it appears that forest-dependent people, who are poor for the most part, constitute a real challenge for development and the environment. A crucial issue is thus to state the conditions under which forest conservation and development can be reconciled. An important factor to consider here is whether agricultural development tends to use land on the intensive or the extensive margin.

Different types of forest use can be elaborated by households, depending essentially on their access to markets. A typology of these strategies is provided by Angelsen and Wunder (2002). First, the *specialized strategy*, related to a high integration into markets, is related to a high contribution of forest products to household income – this strategy fits with the Asia case. Second, the *diversification strategy*, also related to a high integration into markets, only gives a marginal share of income to forest products – this is the case for Latin America. Third, the *coping strategy* is associated with a low share of income from forest products and a low integration into markets. This last strategy does not imply, however, that households do not depend on forests, since they may use forest resources for direct consumption. The coping strategy is often seen in Africa. The first strategy allows an important explicit contribution of forest products to income, with extraction being a main activity of the household. In contrast, the last two strategies give forest product extraction a risk-management role: a relatively low importance in terms of income, but a useful tool to smooth household consumption.

Agricultural expansion, forest products as safety nets and deforestation

Chapter 1 gives an extensive analysis of this insurance use of non-timber forest products (NTFP) by poor households. The representative agricultural household chooses its land use in a manner close to portfolio diversification. Indeed, it faces a simple trade-off: agriculture is more profitable, but risky, while NTFP extraction is safer but less productive. The variables influencing land use are therefore agricultural profitability, NTFP quantities, agricultural risk and risk aversion. In this context, risk reduction may increase deforestation. Indeed, if agricultural risk reduces, households naturally increase the agricultural area and reduce the forest area. For example, the introduction of an insurance or micro-credit mechanism could increase deforestation. In the same manner, if the household becomes less risk-averse, it decreases its NTFP extraction to focus more on agriculture, and thus contributes more to deforestation. Finally, if forests provide a lot of NTFP, the household will keep more land as forests if it uses the diversification strategy.

Commons as insurance: safety nets or poverty traps?

In contrast, Chapter 2 considers the fact that NTFP extraction may have a strong impact on labor allocation. We consider a village economy with no insurance or credit markets. The land use here is considered fixed, which may be consistent in the short run. Households divide their labor allocation between a private project, which provides heterogeneous and risky returns, and extraction from a common-property resource (CPR), which provides homogenous and safe returns. CPR extraction thus has two properties: it constitutes both a minimum income for low-skilled households, and an insurance in case of bad private returns. Three classes of households may thus be distinguished in equilibrium. First, skilled households never use CPR extraction, simply because their private projects always provide enough return, even in the event of economic stress. Second, unskilled households use CPR extraction as a minimum income, because it provides higher returns than their private projects. Finally, middle-class households use CPR extraction as insurance, to ensure a minimum consumption requirement in case of bad private outcome. A poverty trap situation occurs when two much labor is allocated to CPR extraction. In this case, return to labor decreases by a tragedy of the commons effect, and the CPR cannot properly insure the households anymore. Some households thus need to migrate, and the remaining households need to allocate all their labor to the CPR which can only provide them with their minimum requirement. Thus, they are trapped into poverty. In this context, the introduction of an insurance mechanism may help to alleviate poverty and to preserve the resource at the same time.

However, even if poor people are important agents of deforestation and forest degradation, it appears that larger landholders and wealthier economic agents, such as logging firms, also have an important role in forest concerns (World Bank 2006).

National: forest management, corruption and illegal logging

Forests not only constitute a crucial resource for poor households, but are also a harvestable resource at a macro level. Forestry sectors generally represent a small share of national gross domestic product (GDP). In 2000, forestry sectors contributed about 3–5 percent of GDP in Brazil, Guyana,

Suriname, Paraguay, Chile, Latvia, Estonia and some African countries. Overall, forestry sectors contributed 1.5 percent of GDP in Africa, 1.1 percent in western Europe, 1.7 percent in Latin America and 1.2 percent worldwide (Lebedys 2004). Nevertheless, forests employ about 13 million people worldwide and forestry may be the main activity in less developed regions.

Forests can therefore be part of a country's long-term development, but also a source of voracity, rent-seeking behaviors and even crime. Like any other resources, forests require good institutions, sustainable policies and effective enforcement to participate in countries' development without jeopardizing environmental quality.

The issue of corruption is very important in this context. It is a major problem in many developing countries. For instance, the World Bank targets corruption indicators as one of the main elements conditioning international aid. Concerning forest issues, corruption and poor institutions are very important patterns of unsustainable exploitation. It has been estimated that illegal logging induces losses of $10 billion a year in assets and revenue and $5 billion in revenue through tax evasion (Green Building Press 2006). Moreover, illegal logging has important environmental consequences, since it leads to forest over-harvesting, forest degradation and deforestation.

How the size of concessions may influence systemic corruption in forest harvesting: a theoretical assessment

Chapter 3 analyzes the impact of the size of concessions on systemic corruption in the context of forest harvesting. Bureaucratic and policy-maker corruption are considered sequentially. On the one hand, logging firms may bribe bureaucrats so that they underreport harvest volume. Two factors determine the impact of bureaucratic corruption. First, a large number of concessions decreases the individual probability of being inspected by civil agents, and thus creates an incentive to over-harvest. Second, the size of concessions determines the impact of the forest policy on over-harvesting incentives. If the net marginal productivity of effort decreases with the size of concessions, a large number of concessions tends to increase the equilibrium harvest intensity, while a larger number of concessions tends to decrease it. Conversely, a larger number of concessions and a smaller harvested forest tends to increase the equilibrium harvest intensity. Less stringent harvest quotas always increase the equilibrium harvest intensity. On the other hand, a lobby composed of several loggers may bribe the policy-maker so that it designs a less stringent forest policy. A more corrupt policy-maker unsurprisingly designs a more permissive forest policy, that is, a larger number of concessions, a larger harvested forest area and less stringent harvest quota. Considering the links between policy-makers and bureaucratic corruption, this chapter partially supports the idea of systemic corruption. Indeed, policy-maker corruption tends to enhance the impact of bureaucratic corruption through two key policy instruments, and to decrease it through a third. The net impact remains to be determined, but depends crucially on the specification of the loggers' net harvest function, of the welfare function and of the bribe schedule.

Is timber harvesting related to deforestation? On the unsustainable nature of timber harvesting

Chapter 4 investigates empirically the links between forest harvesting and deforestation. Considering that sustainable forest harvesting should not be related to deforestation, our panel-data analysis shows that countries with important timber harvesting tend to deforest more than countries with smaller forest harvesting. This result supports the idea that forest harvesting is mainly unsustainable worldwide. Moreover, this tendency is robust to the addition of corruption and institutions indicators.

It is also shown that countries relying more on timber certification tend to experience lower deforestation rates, which gives the insight that certification is a good indicator of sustainability.

Finally, tropical forests also provide global public services, such as carbon sequestration or biodiversity conservation.

Global: citizen consumption

Forests not only constitute a local resource and environmental indicator, but also have global properties that put the issue on the international agenda. Indeed, as already mentioned, carbon sequestration by forests is an important tool against global warming. Moreover, primary forests are the main biodiversity reservoir. UNESCO lists several forest sites, because of their wildlife wealth, in its World Heritage list (Australia, Brazil, Central African Republic, Democratic Republic of Congo, Indonesia, Kenya, Russia; see whc.unesco.org).

Overall, international organizations appear to be quite involved in forest issues. The FAO has an important forestry department and focuses its work on the economic side of forest issues. The UNEP considers the environmental side of forest issues. The Center for International Forestry Research (CIFOR) is an international research center on forest issues, such as poverty and illegal logging. Nevertheless, even if international organizations get involved in forest conservation and sustainable development, forest issues and deforestation remain an important and alarming environmental concern. Thus, many non-governmental organizations, such as Greenpeace and Friends of the Earth, act to protect forests and denounce illegal logging and corruption. Moreover, individual citizens make a role for themselves, using their economic power to induce more responsible environmental practices. Indeed, consumers are more and more informed of environmental concerns and of marketing and economic practices. Thus, they feel involved in and concerned by the international environment. Two related political consumption practices have emerged in recent years. First, consumer boycotts are a tool commonly and frequently used to induce better corporate environmental practices. Second, ecological certification is now an important signal to consumers sensitive to their environment.

Concerning forest issues, in 2004, WALHI, Indonesia's largest environmental group, and several other environmental groups, called for a boycott of timber from Indonesia, Malaysia, Singapore and China, countries where illegal logging plagues local development and environmental indicators. Moreover, several eco-labels (SmartWood, Scientific Certification Systems, Certified Wood Products Council, Good Wood) certify that timber has been harvested in a sustainable way.

Citizen consumption and public policies: good complements against market failures?

Based on a quotation from the chairman of the Intergovernmental Panel on Climate Change, Chapter 5 considers political consumption in comparison with public policies and weaknesses and complementarities of such behavior. A first conclusion is that political consumption can hardly represent a trustworthy substitute for public policies. Indeed, the idea would be tempting, to assume that if citizens care about the environment, they should just integrate their preferences into their consumption behavior and internalize environmental concerns. If markets are sufficiently reactive, they would necessarily take these preferences into account and a social optimum would somehow be achieved.

However, it is hard to consider that political consumption may be a good substitute for public policies. First, citizen consumers only represent a small share of concerned citizens. Taking, for instance, the case of global warming, consumers from industrialized countries are a marginal part of the whole population. Moreover, most concerned citizens and most probable victims of global warming (say, from the developing South) are not part of this citizen consumption population.

The chapter shows that it would be more efficient to consider political consumption as a complement to public policies. Indeed, government may design conditions under which the influence of citizen consumption may be maximized. Moreover, environmental taxation and subsidies are a potentially efficient way to reduce the cost of green consumption.

On the sources of consumer boycotts ineffectiveness

Chapter 6 aims therefore to analyze the impact of consumer boycotts on firms' practices. Consumer boycotts are considered as a war of attrition between a group of consumers and a targeted firm. Environmentalist consumers refuse to consume the firm's good as long as it is produced with a polluting technology. The boycott is successful if the group of consumers is able to remain in the conflict longer than the firm. Two kinds of characteristics determine the outcome of the game. First, market structure is important. If the market is competitive, it may be open to eco-labeling and certification. Any firm may enter and provide the good with clean production. In this case, boycotting is less costly and the boycott is more likely to succeed. In contrast, if the firm is in a monopoly position, a good substitute is difficult to find, the boycott is more costly and therefore less likely to succeed. Second, demand structure and consumer preferences are important. The boycotting group, that is, the population concerned by the quality of the environment, needs to be quite important, and composed of important consumers. Indeed, the aim of the boycott is to hurt the firm's profit, which means that it should represent an important part of the firm's demand. A simple trade-off therefore describes the problem confronting consumers: boycott by important consumers is very costly for the firm, but boycotting is very costly for those consumers. Finally, coordination failures and free riding are important issues that may jeopardize boycott successes. Overall, consumer boycotts are likely to be quite ineffective.

References

Angelsen, A. and Kaimowitz, D. (1999) Rethinking the causes of deforestation: lessons from economic models. *World Bank Research Observer*, 14(1): 73–98.

Angelsen, A. and Wunder, S. (2002) Exploring the forest-poverty link. CIFOR Occasional Paper no. 40.

FAO (1992) Forest resources assessment, tropical countries. Forestry Paper no. 112, FAO, Rome.

FAO (1997) State of the world forests. Technical report, FAO, Rome.

Green Building Press (2006) Illegal logging dialogue launched in Singapore. http://www.illegal-logging.info/item_single.php?it_id=1682&it=news& printer=1

Lebedys, A. (2004) Trends and current status of the contribution of the forestry sector to national economies. FAO Working Paper FSFM/ACC/07. http://www.fao.org/docrep/007/ad493e/ad493e00.htm (accessed September 26, 2006).

Myers, N. (1992) Tropical forests: the policy challenge. *Environmentalist*, 12(1): 15–27.
Reardon, T., Barret, C., Kelly, V. and Savadogo, K. (1999) Policy reforms and sustainable agricultural intensification in Africa. *Development Policy Review*, 17: 293–313.
Smouts, M. (2002) La deforestation au XXème siècle. *Cahiers Français*, 306.
UNEP (2000) The state of the environment – Africa. In *Geo 2000*. Nairobi: UNEP.
UNEP (2003) Les forêts. In *Geo 2003*. Nairobi: UNEP.
UNEP (2006) *GEO Year Book 2006*. Nairobi: UNEP.
Wollenberg, E. and Ingles, A. E. (1998) *Incomes from the Forest: Methods for the Development and Conservation of Forest Products for Local Communities*. Bogor, Indonesia: Center for International Forestry Research
World Bank (2001) *A revised forest strategy for the World Bank Group*. Technical report, World Bank, Washington DC.
World Bank. (2006) *Strengthening Forest Law Enforcement and Governance: Strengthening a Systemic Constraint to Sustainable Development*. Report No. 36638-GLB. Washington, DC: World Bank.
World Commission on Environment and Development (1987) *Our Common Future*. Oxford: Oxford University Press.

Part II

Local

Forests and people

1 Agricultural expansion, forest products as safety nets and deforestation

This chapter was published in *Environment and Development Economics*, 12(2) (2007).

1.1 Introduction

Among all the causes of tropical deforestation, agricultural expansion appears to be the most important one. Indeed, the share of deforestation related to agricultural expansion has been estimated to be at least 50 percent (FAO 1992; Myers 1992) and at 70 percent in the 1990s (UNEP 2003). In Africa, which is the area with the highest deforestation rates in the world, more than 50 percent of the deforested zones were switched into small exploitations. Deforestation is therefore mostly unplanned and beyond the direct control of governments.

Simultaneously, agricultural development is an important tool for poverty alleviation and long term development (World Bank 2001). Therefore, a crucial question is whether there is a trade-off between rural development and forest conservation. An important factor is the frequent use by poor households of non-timber forest products (NTFP)[1] as safety nets. The consequences of this use for deforestation are an interesting issue and can be investigated with farm household models – a priority for future research (Angelsen and Kaimowitz 1999).

Populations of interest here are farming communities that rely on forest as a supplementary source of income (Byron and Arnold 1999). We consider therefore communities imperfectly integrated into markets. More precisely, imperfections of credit and insurance markets are common in developing countries and especially in rural areas. Indeed, even with informal procedures to insure people and provide credits, studies note high income variabilities (see Townsend 1995; Rosensweig 1988).

Some papers have studied the safety-net role of common property resources, such as forests (Agarwal 1991; Baland and Francois 2005;

Pattanayak and Sills 2001), but they do not consider the impact of this role on the land-use decision. However, households face a trade-off between forest and agriculture. Agriculture can be a way to alleviate poverty, but is a risky activity, while NTFP extraction has low poverty alleviation potential, but is a useful tool to compensate for agricultural risk. This chapter investigates therefore the impact of the use of NTFP as safety nets on the household's decision to increase their agricultural land, and thus, to clear forests.

The safety-net use of NTFP extraction may take two forms, corresponding to two kinds of risk-management strategies. First, the *diversification strategy* is equivalent to a portfolio analysis, because the households use NTFP extraction as a risk-free asset (Aldermann and Paxson 1994). Second, the *coping strategy* consists of extracting NTFP only when agricultural output is too low, working as a "natural" insurance mechanism. Therefore, the problem for the local communities has both the characteristics of portfolio analysis and economics of insurance. The chapter analyzes and compares these diversification and coping strategies. A first comment here is that a diversification strategy is welfare improving compared to a coping strategy, which raises the important question of the risk-management strategy choice. In this chapter, however, the strategies are taken as given and the choice process of the strategy is not considered.

To investigate the impact of the use of NTFP as a risk-management strategy, we build on Angelsen (1999). Our extension allows for agricultural crops uncertainty and for NTFP extraction, neither of which is considered in Angelsen (1999). Thus, the model is an expected utility maximization process of a risk-averse household, which uses forest products to face agricultural crops uncertainty. We assume a community that does not have access to insurance or credit market, so that the risk-management use of forest products is the only way to deal with crop risks.

In this context, the comparative statics show that risk reduction, lower risk aversion, and larger population may be important factors of deforestation for both coping and diversification strategies. In the diversification-strategy case, forest profitability is unambiguously positively correlated with the forest cover. In contrast, in the coping-strategy case, two opposite effects determine the global impact of forest profitability on the forest cover. The *portfolio effect* is a relative profitability effect between agriculture and forests: more land is kept as forests if forests provide a lot of NTFP. The *insurance effect* has the opposite impact: if forests provide a lot of NTFP, less land is needed to insure the households against agricultural crop risks and forest cover is reduced. Finally, a diversification strategy tends to keep more land as forest, by raising the global value of forest products.

Section 1.2 gives a brief review of the literature, emphasizing the use of NTFP for poor agricultural households, describing the economics of land use in agricultural areas and the insurance properties of common property resources. Section 1.3 presents a household model of land-use choice. Section 1.4 addresses some policy implications of the safety-net use of forest products and discusses the possible extensions of the model.

1.2 Review of the literature

1.2.1 The safety-net use of non-timber forest products

In developing countries, about 1.2 billion people rely on agroforestry farming systems that help to sustain agricultural productivity and generate income (World Bank 2001). The risk-management role of forest products is particularly important in the rural systems of developing countries, given that agricultural crops face many risks, such as price shocks, seasonal flooding, unpredictable soil quality, pests, crop diseases or illnesses. NTFP can be used directly in consumption or sold to fill cash gaps. Formally, rural households, which have limited credit and insurance options, choose a diversification of their activities (thus of the land), in order to reduce aggregate risk (Morduch 1995; Godoy *et al.* 2000). Some studies analyze this use of NTFP (Baland and Francois 2005; Pattanayak and Sills 2001). One of the results is that any individual is more likely to visit the forest if the crops are more risky or if he faces a negative shock. Godoy *et al.* (2000), in a study in Honduras, argue that although NTFP extraction has a low annual value, it can provide insurance in the case of unexpected losses. This risk-management role can be particularly important in the case of common risk, because intra-village credit or insurance systems are more difficult to implement (Dercon 2002).

Two risk-management strategies may be implemented (Angelsen and Wunder 2002). The diversification strategy (usually observed in Latin America) is a classic risk-management tool (Aldermann and Paxson 1994). The household raises *ex ante* the number of its activities, choosing if possible activities that have low covariance. In contrast, the coping strategy (observed in Africa) consists in extracting NTFP only in the case of bad agricultural crops. The use of NTFP can here be considered as an *ex post* gap filling use. Forest products are extracted in order to smooth the household's consumption in case of low crop returns.

In these two risk-management approaches, NTFP extraction appears to be efficient for poor rural households. First, a large variety of NTFP can be extracted, thus raising the diversification of activities. Several studies mention fuel, fodder, fibres, oil seeds, edible fruits, staple foods, vegetables, spices, rope, leaf-plates, medicinal plants, vines, honey, sap, Brazilian nuts, fruits bark and rubber (see Kumar 2002, for rural India; Pattanayak and Sills

2001, for the Tapajos National Forest, Brazilian Amazon). Second, many NTFP do not have strong positive correlation among themselves or with agricultural output (Pattayanak and Sills 2001), so that they can be efficient risk-management instruments. A bad agricultural output is not necessarily linked to bad forest product quantities.

Two characteristics of NTFP are important to note. First, there are low capital and skills requirements for NTFP extraction as well as open or semi-open access to the resource, so that poor households can easily extract the resource. Neumann and Hirsch (2000) argue that the poorest people are those who are most engaged in NTFP extraction. Second, NTFP habitually have low returns to labor, so that they have poor potential to alleviate poverty (Wunder 2001; Angelsen and Wunder 2002). Studying Bagyeli and Bantu communities in South Cameroon, Van Dijk (in Ros-Tonen and Wiersum 2003) gives an illustration of the relatively low share of NTFP in total income – which argues for the risk-management strategie – and of the link between poverty and NTFP use.

Hence, forests are competing for land use, with agricultural use representing the most important alternative. Indeed, forest products have a low potential of poverty alleviation, but can be used to compensate shortfalls in agricultural yields. Conversely, agricultural crops is a potential way out of poverty for households, but may represent a high level of risk, especially if the households have low access to insurance or credit markets. The trade-off between these two land uses is a major choice for poor rural households, and is a potentially driving force of deforestation. An interesting topic is thus to analyze the land-use choice process of households.

1.2.2   The land-use choice with NTFP extraction

Among the papers that study land-use choice by rural communities, only a few take into account the forest product use, and none study the risk-management use described here. Lopez (1998) notes the coexistence in most developing countries of private lands, intended for agricultural crops, and common property lands, namely forests, used for their products. In his paper, however, the two land uses compete with each other and forest products extraction is not a risk-management strategy. Specifically, Lopez analyzes the consequences of agricultural intensification and farm productivity improvement programs on the pressures on the common resource. The main factor determining the programs' impact on pressure on the common resource is the factor-intensity of the crops. If crops are labor-intensive, then a rise in their prices is likely to diminish the pressure on the common resource. However, if crops are land-intensive, the pressure is likely to rise with the commodity prices.

Parks *et al.* (1998) study the competing land uses, mainly agriculture, timber and non-timber forest products. The paper distinguishes four cases, depending on the relative productivity of the different activities: joint management of forests, forest preservation, conversion to non-forest use, and forest abandonment. These four cases depend mainly on the impact of the age of the trees and the management effort on a profit maximization function.

1.2.3 Common property resources as safety net

The literature on land-use choice discussed above ignores the safety-net role that forests have when they are commonly held. Another part of the literature does, however, argue the importance of common property resources (CPR) as safety net. Baland and Francois (2005) find a negative impact of land privatization on the social welfare of a community. CPR represent for low-skilled households a potential outside option to private projects, since CPR extraction often requires low-skilled labor.

Pattanayak and Sills (2001) find that NTFP collection is positively correlated with agricultural shortfall and expected agricultural risk. According to Bromley and Chavas (1989), non-exclusive property rights can be seen as an integral part of risk sharing. In this case, the common forest can be considered as an asset of last resort (Baland and Francois 2005). A strong link between poor people and CPR is often underlined. Dasgupta and Maler (1993) argue that local commons provide the rural poor with partial protection in time of unusual economic stress. A study of tribal groups in rural Bihar qualifies communally-held forests as the only means of survival for poorer members in lean seasons (Agrawal 1991). Reddy and Chakravaty (1999) observe in India a more intensive use of the CPR by poor households. Dasgupta (1987) notes a higher level of CPR products in low labor productivity regions. Jodha (1986) finds a negative relationship between CPR income and rural inequalities.

Although some papers study the competing land-use relationship between agriculture and forests, none of them investigate the safety-net use of forest products to insure against crops risk. In contrast, papers studying the safety-net role of CPR treat the share private/common land as exogenous. The aim of this chapter is thus to reconcile these two sides of the literature, investigating the role of the safety-net use of NTFP on the land-use choice.

1.3 Diversification strategy, risk-aversion and the household's optimal land use

The model presented is an adaptation from Angelsen (1999). In contrast to Angelsen's setup, agricultural output is uncertain and forest provides NTFP that are used to smooth the household's consumption.

THE SETUP FOR THE LAND

The model represents a village economy. The total area of the village is normalized to 1. We assume here only two possible uses for the land: agriculture and forests. Both agricultural and forested areas are assumed to have the same quality. In contrast to Angelsen (1999), we assume here that the forests provide NTFP. We assume here for simplicity an egalitarian repartition of the land across the households in the village. Therefore, we consider a representative household, which has a share $\frac{1}{N}$ of the total area of the village (N is the number of households in the village and is our indicator of population pressure), which is equivalent to a share $\frac{1}{N}$ of total forest product extraction. We avoid thus the problem of the tragedy of the commons, i.e. competition between households for the forest products. We also assume that both the agricultural good and the forest product are homogeneous. For both goods, land and labor are the only inputs. We assume that the household uses an optimal combination of labor in the production process. Thus, the labor side is not explicitly considered here. The implicit assumption is that the household's labor force is entirely used and that the household may eventually hire outside labor.[2]

R is the share of agricultural land in the village area ($0 \leq R \leq 1$). Agricultural land area used by the household is thus defined as $\frac{R}{N}$ and forest land area for household use is $\frac{1-R}{N}$. R is an indicator of the agricultural land cover and the choice variable of the household. At the beginning of the period, the household chooses the share of the land it will cultivate. If $R = 1$, all the land around the village is converted to agriculture and deforestation is maximized in the village area. If $R = 0$, forest conservation is maximized and there is no agriculture. Between these two extreme cases, there is a trade-off between the two possible uses of the land.

THE SAFETY-NET USE OF FOREST PRODUCTS

We focus here on the diversification strategy. The setup corresponding to the coping strategy is provided in Appendix 1B. In the coping case, we assume that NTFP extraction only happens if the agricultural crop output is low. We assume that agricultural land is, on average, more profitable than forest land, but agricultural production is more volatile than NTFP. Thus, there is a trade-off between a relatively more profitable but riskier activity – agriculture – and a relatively less profitable but safer activity – NTFP extraction. In contrast to Angelsen (1999), the agricultural output is not certain. The risk on agricultural crops is supposed to be systemic. Therefore, every household in the village lives in the same state of the world. Thus, there cannot be inter-household insurance.

There are two states of the world. In the good state, which occurs with probability δ, the agricultural output per hectare (or per unit of land, as the area is normalized to 1) is high:

$$\overline{C} \equiv \frac{1}{N}[R\bar{x} + (1-R)f] \tag{1.1}$$

where $\bar{x}$ is the optimal agricultural output (net of costs) per hectare in the good state of the world. f is the quantity of forest products extracted per hectare, net of extraction costs. In contrast to the agricultural output, f is assumed to be certain.

In the bad state, with probability $1 - \delta$, agricultural output is low:

$$\underline{C} \equiv \frac{1}{N}[R\underline{x} + (1-R)f] \tag{1.2}$$

where $\underline{x}$ is the optimal agricultural output in the bad state of the world. Clearly $\underline{x} < \bar{x}$ must hold. Expected agricultural output per hectare is therefore:

$$E(x) = \delta\bar{x} + (1-\delta)\underline{x} \tag{1.3}$$

Clearly, by assumption $f < E(x)$, for otherwise there is no trade-off between the two land uses and all the land is used for forest product extraction.

1.3.1 Expected utility maximization

The objective of the household is to maximize its expected utility. Then the household's utility function only depends on consumption: $U = U(C)$, with $\frac{\partial U}{\partial C} > 0$. Expected utility is then:

$$E(U) = E_U(E_c; \sigma_c^2) \tag{1.4}$$

The expected level of consumption of the household is E_c and its variance is σ_c^2. We have $\frac{\partial E_U}{\partial E_c} > 0$ and $\frac{\partial E_U}{\partial \sigma_c^2} < 0$. If we do not specify the utility function, the expected utility is likely to depend on the other moments. We do not consider, however, this case here. This framework is thus consistent with a quadratic utility function or with a constant absolute risk aversion (CARA) function. We thus introduce a CARA function, with α being the Arrow–Pratt absolute risk aversion coefficient:

$$U(C) = -\exp[-\alpha C] \tag{1.5}$$

MEAN–VARIANCE ANALYSIS

Both the expected level of consumption and its variance depend on the share of agricultural land, R, to be chosen by the household. Expected utility is then

$$E_U = -\delta \, \exp[-\alpha \bar{C}] - (1 - \delta) \exp[-\alpha \underline{C}] \tag{1.6}$$

where expected consumption and variance do not appear explicitly.

The household can either consume directly what it produces or sell it to purchase other goods. Thus, we consider the equality between consumption and production as a budget constraint. The expected level of consumption is therefore

$$E_c(R) = \frac{1}{N}[R(E(x) - f) + f], \quad \frac{\partial E_c(R)}{\partial R} > 0 \tag{1.7}$$

Expected consumption rises with the share of agricultural land, R, since expected agricultural production is more efficient than forest product extraction. Therefore, a risk-neutral household would convert all the land into fields ($R = 1$) in order to maximize its expected consumption. The variance of consumption is

$$\sigma_c^2 = \frac{1}{N^2}\sigma_x^2 R^2$$

If NTFP extraction is impossible, the only way to have no variance in consumption is to have $R = 0$, with $E_c(R) = 0$. Diversification does not change the relationship between the variance of consumption and R, but having a positive expected consumption with no variance is possible, fixing $R = 0$. In contrast, the introduction of a coping strategy allows for a positive expected consumption with no variance. In this case, the variance of consumption is minimized (as σ_c^2 is a convex function of R) and zero if:

$$R = \frac{f}{\bar{x} - \underline{x} + f} \equiv \underline{R} \tag{1.8}$$

$\underline{R}$ is thus a lower bound for R, in the coping-strategy case. Indeed, for $R < \underline{R}$, expected utility is increasing in R. The household is clearly better off with NTFP extraction. Its expected level of consumption increases and there can be no uncertainty about the level of consumption. Moreover, the

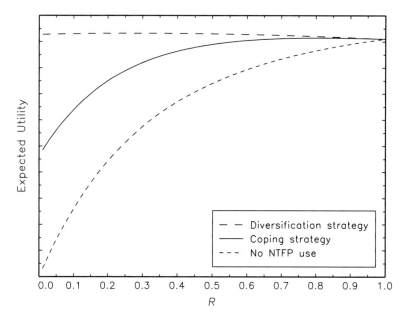

Figure 1.1 Expected utility as a function of *R*, *Parameters: App.C.*

diversification strategy is more welfare improving than the coping strategy, as it raises the households' utility in each state of the world (see Figure 1.1). This fact raises the question of the motivations that lead a household to apply the coping strategy instead of the diversification strategy. Potential explanations include seasonality, labor allocation, labor/leisure arbitrage and difference in utility between NTFP and the agricultural good.

This chapter does not take into account those potential factors, and thus considers the strategy as given. Moreover, the model presented here suggests the same timing for both diversification and coping strategy. This assumption is quite artificial, because diversification is an *ex ante* strategy, while coping is done *ex post*. The setup presented here thus fits better with the diversification case. One therefore needs to be very careful when considering the coping case results and comparing with the diversification case, as a different timing may lead to different conclusions.

The choice of land use is a trade-off between expected consumption and variance of consumption. The relative weight given to the expected consumption and the variance will depend on its risk aversion: a risk-averse household gives more importance to the variance of consumption than a risk-neutral household.

HOUSEHOLD'S OBJECTIVE AND THE OPTIMAL TRADE-OFF

The objective of the household is to choose R in order to maximize expected utility

$$\max_{R} \; E_U(E_c(R), \sigma_c^2(R)) \tag{1.9}$$

Note that $\frac{\partial E_U}{\partial R} > 0$ if $f \leq \underline{x}$. Therefore, we have a corner solution ($R = 1$) if the forest profitability is lower than or equal to the agricultural profitability in the bad state of the world. In this framework, the safety-net use of the forest products only exists if the risk on agricultural output is so high that NTFP extraction becomes the main activity of the household in the bad state of the world. This condition is consistent with a portfolio analysis, where the risk-free asset needs to be more profitable than the risky asset in some states of the world to have a positive share in the portfolio (Gollier 2001). We now characterize the agricultural frontier that maximizes expected utility. The first-order condition gives the optimal agricultural frontier

$$R^* = \left(\frac{N \left[\ln \frac{\delta(\bar{x} - f)}{(1-\delta)(f - \underline{x})} \right]}{\alpha(\bar{x} - \underline{x})} \right) \tag{1.10}$$

1.3.2 Comparative statics

In this framework of risk on agricultural output, we define risk reduction as a rise in $\underline{x}$ and a fall in $\bar{x}$, with a constant expected output $E(x)$. This kind of risk reduction can be viewed as the introduction of an insurance system. On the one hand, the household pays a risk premium $d\bar{x}$ per hectare in the good state of the world. On the other hand, if the bad state of the world occurs, the household receives as insurance $d\underline{x}$ per hectare. This risk reduction definition implies $(1 - \delta)d\underline{x} = -\delta d\bar{x}$, with $d\underline{x} > 0$.

PROPOSITION 1.1 *Risk reduction, lower risk aversion and larger population decrease the forest cover, both with the diversification and coping strategies.*

Proof: Sign of the first derivatives of R^* (see Appendices 1A and 1B): $\left(\frac{\partial R^*}{\partial \underline{x}} - \frac{(1-\delta)}{\delta} \frac{\partial R^*}{\partial \bar{x}} \right) > 0$, $\frac{\partial R^*}{\partial \alpha} < 0$ and $\frac{\partial R^*}{\partial N} > 0$. □

Risk reduction has a positive impact on R. Hence, if the agricultural risk is reduced, the safety-net use of NTFP is less important, agricultural land increases and forest cover declines. Intuitively, if the more profitable activity becomes less risky – with the same expected profitability – its share in the agent's portfolio rises. In our example, the introduction of an insurance mechanism thus leads to more deforestation.

The Arrow–Pratt absolute risk aversion coefficient has a positive impact on the forest cover. Intuitively, if the household is risk averse, it keeps more land as forest in order to insure itself against crop risks, even if this is done at the expense of lower expected consumption.

The village population has a negative impact on the forest cover (positive impact on R). Indeed, a larger population reduces the size allowed to each household. Each household therefore raises the share of the most profitable activity.

PROPOSITION 1.2 *Considering the diversification strategy, the forest profitability tends to increase the forest cover. Considering the coping strategy, two opposite effects determine the impact of forest profitability on the forest cover. A portfolio effect tends to increase the forest cover, while an insurance effect tends to reduce it.*

Proof: For the diversification case, the sign of the first derivative is unambiguously negative (Appendix 1A). For the coping case, the sign of the first derivative of R^* with respect to f is not determined, and two components can be distinguished (see Appendix 1B). ☐

In the diversification case, consistently with a portfolio analysis, the portfolio share of the risk-free asset, i.e. NTFP extraction, is positively correlated with its profitability. The coping case is slightly different. First, if the forest profitability increases, its relative profitability rises, which tends to increase the forest cover. We call this effect the *portfolio effect*: the share of the risk-free asset – NTFP extraction – in the agent's portfolio is positively correlated with its profitability. Second, if the forest provides a lot of NTFP, less land is needed to insure the household. This *insurance effect* tends to reduce the forest cover when the forest is more profitable, and to increase the most profitable activity. The relative importance of the portfolio and insurance effects depends on risk aversion. A highly risk-averse household will give less importance to the portfolio effect. A rise in forest profitability could come, for example, from a rise in the NTFP prices. A policy frequently advocated to reduce tropical deforestation is the introduction of green labeling for NTFP in order to raise the profitability of the forests. However, this positive impact on the forest cover is not straightforward: if the households use the coping strategy and are highly risk averse, the insurance effect may dominate and the introduction of green labeling would reduce forest cover. Appendix 1C provides a numerical example of the coping and diversification strategies.

1.4 Conclusion

This chapter aims to investigate the safety-net function of forest products in the economics of land-use change and deforestation. We analyze the trade-off between two land uses. Agriculture is more profitable but is risky. In contrast, NTFP extraction is less profitable but is used to fill some consumption gaps when agricultural crops are bad.

The model presented ignores some important features of poor agricultural households, which opens up opportunities for future research. First, the households may compete for NTFP extraction if the forest is open access. The potential poverty-trap implications that NTFP extraction may create must then be taken into account. Indeed, if the population in need of a safety net is large, and if the forest capacity is small, a tragedy-of-the-commons process may trap the less skilled households into NTFP extraction and deprive them of other development opportunities. Second, considering more explicitly labor market integration could point outside opportunities for households, that would reduce the safety-net role of NTFP extraction and thus increase deforestation. Third, other types of risk management could have several implications for land use. For example, agricultural households could use livestock as a risk-management strategy, which could increase land clearing and deforestation. Fourth, the statement of risk-free NTFP extraction should be moderated, because of the existence of risk such as animal migration or price volatility. Finally, in the setting presented here, a risk-diversification strategy is clearly more welfare improving (but less forest saving) than a risk-coping strategy, which raises the important question about the factors that motivate the use of coping strategies instead of diversification strategies. Concerning this last point, the setup used here describes probably better the diversification case, because it is an *ex ante* strategy. A more precise timing, including seasonality, would thus give a more accurate description of the coping case.

However, although quite simple and not considering some important factors such as dynamic effects or labor allocation, the model presented here stresses some important implications. We predict that a reduction in crop risk may have a negative impact on forest cover. Development policies often consider agricultural development as a priority. Moreover, an important objective is to reduce the risk on poor agricultural households' income. Therefore, to reduce this impact, risk reduction policies should be combined with environmental and forest management policies. For example, payment for environmental services provided by forests may be an interesting tool. Indeed, this kind of payment may enhance forest preservation and raise the "profitability" of forests.

Risk aversion of the household is positively correlated with forest cover. This result is quite intuitive, since forest products are a tool to reduce risk. In the economic analysis, households are typically more risk averse than entrepreneurs, generally risk neutral. Economic development may raise through market integration the separability between the utility- and profit-maximizing process. The risk aversion of the household may fall, which could have a negative impact on forest cover. Moreover, market integration should provide households new insurance and credit mechanisms, reducing the safety-net use of forest products described in this chapter. This kind of market integration can thus indirectly lead to more deforestation.

Appendix 1A: Comparative statics – the risk-averse household model

Proof of Proposition 1.1: We take the first derivatives of the optimal share of agricultural land R^* with respect to our variables of interest. We define a risk reduction as a rise in $\underline{x}$ and a fall in $\bar{x}$, with a constant expected output $E(x)$: $(1 - \delta)d\underline{x} + \delta d\bar{x} = 0$; $d\underline{x} > 0$; $d\bar{x} < 0$.

$$\left(\frac{\partial R^*}{\partial \underline{x}} - \frac{1 - \delta}{\delta} \frac{\partial R^*}{\partial \bar{x}} \right) \cdot d\underline{x}$$

$$= N \frac{\left[\ln\left(\frac{\delta(\bar{x}-f)}{(1-\delta)(f-\underline{x})} \right) + \frac{(\bar{x}-\underline{x})(E(x)-f)}{(\bar{x}-f)(f-\underline{x})} \right]}{\delta\alpha(\bar{x} - \underline{x})^2} \cdot d\underline{x} > 0 \tag{1.11}$$

$$\frac{\partial R^*}{\partial \alpha} = \frac{-N \ln\left[\frac{\delta(\bar{x}-f)}{(1-\delta)(f-\underline{x})} \right]}{\alpha^2[\bar{x} - \underline{x}]} < 0 \tag{1.12}$$

$$\frac{\partial R^*}{\partial N} = \frac{\ln\left[\frac{\delta(\bar{x}-f)}{(1-\delta)(f-\underline{x})} \right]}{\alpha[\bar{x} - \underline{x}]} > 0 \tag{1.13}$$

Proof of Proposition 1.2: Forest profitability has a positive impact on the forest cover:

$$\frac{\partial R^*}{\partial f} = \frac{N}{\alpha(\bar{x} - \underline{x})} \left[\frac{-1}{(\bar{x} - f)} - \frac{1}{(f - \underline{x})} \right] < 0 \tag{1.14}$$

Appendix 1B: NTFP as a risk-coping strategy

This appendix aims to stress the differences between the coping and the diversification strategies. The only difference with the diversification strategy is that NTFP are extracted only when agricultural output is bad. All the changes in the results come from this difference.

1B.1 Changes in the main model results

$$E(f) = (1 - \delta)f \tag{1.15}$$

$$\bar{C} = \frac{1}{N}R\bar{x} \tag{1.16}$$

$$\underline{C} = \frac{1}{N}[R\underline{x} + (1 - R)f] \tag{1.17}$$

$$E_c(R) = \delta\bar{C} + (1 - \delta)\underline{C} = \frac{1}{N}[R(E(x) - E(f)) + E(f)] \tag{1.18}$$

$$\sigma_c^2 = E(C^2) - E(C)^2 = \left(\frac{1}{N}\right)^2[R\sigma_x - (1 - R)\sigma_f]^2 \tag{1.19}$$

$$R^* = \left(\frac{f + \frac{N}{\alpha}\left[\ln\frac{\delta\bar{x}}{(1-\delta)(f-\underline{x})}\right]}{\bar{x} - \underline{x} + f}\right) \tag{1.20}$$

1B.2 Comparative statics

Proof of Proposition 1.1: As in the risk-diversification case, risk reduction, lower risk aversion and larger population decrease the forest cover:

$$\left(\frac{\partial R^*}{\partial \underline{x}} - \frac{1 - \delta}{\delta}\frac{\partial R^*}{\partial \bar{x}}\right) \cdot d\underline{x}$$

$$= \frac{f + \frac{N}{\alpha}\left[\ln\left(\frac{\delta\bar{x}}{(1-\delta)(f-\underline{x})}\right) + \frac{(E(x)-(1-\delta)f)(\bar{x}-\underline{x}+f)}{\bar{x}(f-\underline{x})}\right]}{\delta(\bar{x} - \underline{x} + f)^2} \cdot d\underline{x} > 0 \tag{1.21}$$

$$\frac{\partial R^*}{\partial \alpha} = \frac{-N\ln\left[\frac{\delta\bar{x}}{(1-\delta)(f-\underline{x})}\right]}{\alpha^2[\bar{x} - \underline{x} + f]} < 0 \tag{1.22}$$

$$\frac{\partial R^*}{\partial N} = \frac{\ln\left[\frac{\delta\bar{x}}{(1-\delta)(f-\underline{x})}\right]}{\alpha[\bar{x} - \underline{x} + f]} > 0 \tag{1.23}$$

Proof of Proposition 1.2: The sign of the derivative of R^* with respect to f is not determined:

$$\frac{\partial R^*}{\partial f} = \frac{\bar{x} - \underline{x} - \frac{N}{\alpha}\left[1 + \frac{\bar{x}}{f-\underline{x}} + \ln\left[\frac{\delta\bar{x}}{(1-\delta)(f-\underline{x})}\right]\right]}{(\bar{x} - \underline{x} + f)^2} \tag{1.24}$$

However, two opposite effects can be distinguished. First, the insurance effect pushes up the agricultural share and depends on the gap between agricultural profitability in the two states $(\bar{x} - \underline{x})$. Second, the portfolio effect tends to increase the forest cover and depends on the relative profitability of forests compared to agriculture in the two states of the world $(1 + \frac{\bar{x}}{f - \underline{x}} + \ln[\frac{\delta \bar{x}}{(1 - \delta)(f - \underline{x})}])$. Note that the portfolio effect is decreasing in risk aversion α.

Appendix 1C: A numerical illustration

The values of the variables (Table 1.1) are adapted from Angelsen (1995, 1999). They correspond as far as possible to a household survey done in the Seberida district, Riau, Sumatra. For the variables not corresponding to the survey (i.e. δ, $\bar{x}$, $\underline{x}$, f, and α), we use values corresponding to the basic conditions of the model ((1.3), (1.2)). In the coping case, we see that the portfolio effect dominates the insurance effect here (Table 1.2). Note that, for $\alpha > 1.52$, the insurance effect is bigger than the portfolio effect, and

Table 1.1 Parameter values of the numerical simulation

Variable	Symbol	Initial value	Adapted value
Total land area	H	1932	1
Number of households	N	82	0.042
Expected output in agriculture	$E(x)$	500	0.26
Low level of output	$\underline{x}$	n.a	0.15
High level of output	$\bar{x}$	n.a	0.37
Forest products intensity	f	n.a	0.22
Probability of $\bar{x}$	δ	n.a	0.5
Absolute risk aversion coefficient	α	n.a	0.5

n.a.: not available.
Source: Angelsen (1995, 1999).

Table 1.2 Results of the numerical simulation

	Change in parameters	Coping	Diversification
Initial situation	cf. Table 1.1	0.82	0.29
Risk reduction	$\bar{x} = 0.36$; $\underline{x} = 0.16$	0.88	0.36
Forest profitability	$f = 0.2$	0.88	0.47
	$f = 0.24$	0.78	0.14
Risk aversion	$\alpha = 0.3$	1	0.48
	$\alpha = 0.7$	0.73	0.21

a rise in f decreases the forest cover. The diversification strategy tends to keep more land as forests than the coping strategy.

References

Agarwal, B. (1991) Social security and the family: coping with seasonality and calamity in rural India. In E. Ahmad, J. Dreze, J. Hills, and A. Sen (eds), *Social Security in Developing Countries*. Oxford: Clarendon Press, pp. 171–244.

Alderman, H. and Paxson, C. H. (1994) Do the poor insure? A synthesis of the literature on risk and consumption in developing countries. In D. Bacha (ed.), *Economics in a Changing World*, Vol. 3. London: Macmillan, pp. 48–78.

Angelsen, A. (1995) Shifting cultivation and deforestation: A study from Indonesia. *World Development*, 23(10).

Angelsen, A. (1999) Agricultural expansion and deforestation: Modelling the impact of population, market forces and property rights. *Journal of Development Economics*, 58: 185–218.

Angelsen, A. and Kaimowitz, D. (1999) Rethinking the causes of deforestation: Lessons from economic models'. *World Bank Research Observer*, 14(1): 73–98.

Angelsen, A. and Wunder, S. (2002) Exploring the forest-poverty link. CIFOR Occasional Paper no. 40.

Baland, J. and Francois, P. (2005) Commons as insurance and the welfare impact of privatization. *Journal of Public Economics*, 89(2–3): 211–31.

Bluffstone, R. (1995) The effect of labor market performance on deforestation in developing countries under open access: An example from rural Nepal. *Journal of Environmental Economics and Management*, 29: 42–63.

Bromley, D. and Chavas, J. (1989) On risk, transactions and economic development in the semiarid tropics. *Economic Development and Cultural Change*, 37: 719–36.

Byron, N. and Arnold, M. (1997) What future for the people of the tropical forests?' CIFOR Working Paper no. 19.

Dasgupta, M. (1987) Informal security mechanisms and population retention in rural India. *Economic Development and Cultural Change*, 36(1): 101–20.

Dasgupta, P. and Mäler, K.-G. (1993) Poverty, institutions and the environmental resource base. In J. Behrman and T.N. Srinavasan (eds), *Handbook of Development Economics*, Vol. 3. Amsterdam: North-Holland.

Dercon, S. (2002) Income risk, coping strategies and safety nets. *World Bank Research Observer*, 17(2): 141–66.

FAO (1992) Forest resources assessment, tropical countries. Forestry Paper no. 112, FAO, Rome.

Godoy, R., Wilke, D., Overman, H., Cubas, A., Cubas, G., Demmer, J., McSweeney, K. and Brokaw, N. (2000) Valuation of consumption and sale of forest goods from a Central American rain forest. *Nature*, 406(6): 62–3.

Gollier, C. (2001) *The Economics of Risk and Time*. Cambridge, MA: MIT Press.

Jodha, N. (1986) Common property resources and rural poor in dry regions of India. *Economic and Political Weekly*, 21(27): 1169–81.

Kumar, S. (2002) Does participation in common pool resource management help the poor? A social cost-benefit analysis of joint forest management in Jharkland, India. *World Development*, 30(5): 763–82.

Lopez, R. (1998) Agricultural intensification, common property resources and the farm-household'. *Environmental and Resource Economics*, 11(3–4).

Morduch, J. (1995) Income smoothing and consumption smoothing. *Journal of Economic Perspectives, American Economic Association*, 9(3): 103–14.

Myers, N. (1992) Tropical forests: The policy challenge *Environmentalist*, 12(1): 15–27.

Neumann, R. and Hirsch, E. (2000) Commercialisation of non-timber forest products: a review. Technical report, CIFOR, Bogor, Indonesia and FAO, Rome.

Parks, P., Barbie, E. and Burgess, J. (1998) The economics of forest land use in temperate and tropical areas. *Environmental and Resource Economics*, 11(3–4): 473–87.

Pattanayak, S. and Sills, E. (2001) Do tropical forests provide natural insurance? The microeconomics of non-timber forest product collection in the Brazilian Amazon. *Land Economics*, 77(4): 595–612.

Reddy, S. and Chakravaty, S. (1999) Forest dependence and income distribution in a subsistence economy. *World Development*, 27(7): 1141–9.

Ros-Tonen, M. and Wiersum, F. (2003) The importance of non-timber forest products for forest-based rural livelihoods: an evolving research agenda. AGIDS.

Rosenzweig, M. (1988) Risk, implicit contracts and the family in rural areas of low-income countries. *Economic Journal*, 98: 1148–70.

Townsend, R. (1995) Consumption insurance: an evaluation of risk-bearing systems in low-income economies. *Journal of Economic Perspectives*, 9(3): 83–102.

UNEP (2003) Les forêts. In *Geo 2003*. Nairobi: UNEP.

WorldBank (2001) A revised forest strategy for the World Bank group. Technical report, World Bank, Washington D.C.

Wunder, S. (2001) Poverty alleviation and tropical forests. What scope for synergies? *World Development*, 29(11): 1817–33.

2 Commons as insurance

Safety nets or poverty traps?

This chapter was published in *Environment and Development Economics*, 14(3) (2009).

2.1 Introduction

The aim of this chapter is to highlight the potential poverty-trap implications of a common property resource (CPR) used as insurance. Several case studies have considered the insurance role of commonly held resources, such as forests, commonly held lands, or fisheries. Indeed, in many developing countries, credit and insurance markets are incomplete, and weaknesses of the welfare state often coincide with poverty and high inequalities. In this case, CPR extraction appears to be an important risk-management strategy for poor households.

Taking the example of non-timber forest products (NTFP) extraction in open-access forests, Angelsen and Wunder (2002) wonder if this activity constitutes a poverty trap for poorer households. Indeed, NTFP extraction habitually has low return to labor, so that it has poor potential to alleviate poverty (Wunder 2001; Angelsen and Wunder 2002). Moreover, Neumann and Hirsch (2000) argue that the poorest people are those who are most engaged in NTFP extraction. NTFP extraction has therefore both the advantage of offering to poor households an activity to survive, with the disadvantage of keeping them in poverty.

Thus, considering how a CPR constitutes both a safety net and a poverty trap is an important issue, because it concerns both the population's welfare and the quality of the environment. Azariadis and Stachuski (2005) define a poverty trap as a "self reinforcing mechanism which causes poverty to persist". We consider here that a poverty trap is a situation in which households do not get more than their subsistence requirement, while more lucrative, but riskier, opportunities are available. We differ therefore from the usual poverty trap applications, which involve dynamics and multiple equilibria.

In the context studied here, CPR extraction has both properties of offering minimum income to low-skilled households and insurance. Indeed, some households mix their labor allocation between risk-free CPR extraction and a risky but more profitable activity. As an extreme case, since the average return to CPR extraction is decreasing with total labor allocated, households need to allocate all their labor to the CPR to be properly insured. A poverty trap is considered as a situation in which households cannot get more than their subsistence requirement from their activities, while more profitable outside options are available. Households are trapped in CPR extraction activity because of their need for insurance, which keeps them away from other development opportunities.

Thus, CPR extraction may constitute a poverty trap as a result of a tragedy-of-the-commons process. Too many households are in need of insurance and the resource cannot provide enough to properly insure all the population. They face thus the classic poverty–environment nexus, where poor people depend too much on their environment and overuse it. Therefore, analyzing this type of situation may highlight win–win opportunities to improve the welfare of populations and preserve the environment at the same time. For example, introducing inter-household or private insurance or credit mechanisms may relax pressure on the resource and be a partial solution to the poverty trap.

Section 2.2 gives a brief review of the case studies investigating the insurance role of the commons. Section 2.3 presents the insurance role of CPR extraction and Section 2.4 derives the conditions under which CPR extraction constitutes both a safety net and a poverty trap. Sections 2.5 and 2.6 investigate the impact of the introduction of cooperative and private insurance mechanisms, respectively. Section 2.7 concludes and discusses potential policy implications.

2.2   Insurance properties of common resources

In the case of market incompleteness, commonly held resources are frequently used as an insurance tool by poor households. Pattanayak and Sills (2001) find a positive correlation between NTFP collection, agricultural shortfall, and expected agricultural risk. According to Bromley and Chavas (1989), non-exclusive property rights can be seen as an integral part of risk sharing. In this case, common forests can be considered as an asset of last resort (Baland and Francois 2005). A strong link between poor people and CPR is often underlined. Dasgupta and Mäler (1993) argue that local commons provide the rural poor with partial protection in time of unusual economic stress. A study of tribal groups in rural Bihar qualifies communally held forests as the only means of survival for poorer members in lean seasons (Agrawal 1991). Reddy and Chakravaty (1999) observe in India a more intensive use of CPR by poor households. Dasgupta (1987) notes a higher level of CPR products in low labor productivity regions. Jodha (1986) finds a negative relationship between CPR income and rural inequalities.

Baland and Francois (2005) analyze the insurance property of a CPR, and compare it with the increased efficiency if this resource is privatized. In their paper, each household has the choice between two activities: CPR extraction and a private project. CPR extraction requires low-skilled labor, which implies homogeneous returns for labor. The private projects provide heterogeneous returns, depending on the household skills. Therefore, CPR extraction represents for low-skilled households an outside option to private project, while the most skilled households allocate their labor to the private projects. The authors found a potential negative impact of the resource privatization on the welfare of the community's poorest members.

Most papers agree on the fact that CPR extraction is an important risk-management tool, especially for poorer households; Wunder (2002) notes the low development potential of NTFP extraction, and Angelsen *et al.* (2001) argue that relying too much on this activity may lead to a poverty trap. Building on Baland and Francois (2005), the following model shows the mechanism that leads a CPR when used as insurance to becoming a poverty trap. A poverty trap refers here to a situation in which households are trapped in an activity that cannot provide more than their subsistence requirements, while there exist more profitable outside options. In this context, a cooperative shift in labor allocation may sustain other equilibria, bringing households out of poverty. The introduction of private insurance may also be a potential solution to the problem.

Although the literature on CPR insurance properties is quite developed, very few papers analyze the impact of the introduction of insurance mechanisms or microcredit on CPR extraction. First, Godoy *et al.* (1997), in a study on Amerindian households in Honduras, note that households with stronger credit constraints tend to use forests resources more intensively. McSweeney (2005) finds that households with cattle and other types of belongings used less forest resources when Hurricane Mitch occurred. Indeed, these households may sell those belongings in order to smooth consumption, and thus do not need the insurance properties provided by common forests. McSweeney (2003), in a study on indigenous households of the Tawahka Asangni Biosphere Reserve (Nicaragua), finds that the households able to borrow money from their relatives tend not to use NTFP extraction. Finally, Anderson *et al.* (2002), citing several microcredit institutions opinion, argue that the introduction of microcredit should decrease forest over-exploitation. However, the authors note the lack of case studies and empirical analysis on the impact of microcredit introduction on CPR use.

The following sections present a simple model of CPR extraction used as insurance that may lead to poverty trap situations.

2.3 Commons as insurance

Building on Baland and Francois (2005), we consider a second-best economy, with no insurance and no credit market. The N households of the community allocate their unit of labor between two activities. First, labor can be allocated to a private project (e.g. private agriculture). Second, it can be allocated to CPR extraction (e.g. NTFP extraction from commonly held forests). Each household can divide its labor and allocate a share to both activities.

Baland and Francois consider successively a risk-free private project with heterogeneous returns, and a risky private project with homogeneous returns. Conversely, we consider here a risky private project with heterogeneous returns, while CPR extraction provides safe and homogeneous returns. Therefore, CPR extraction may have two motivations. First, households have different expected returns on their private project, and less skilled households allocate all their labor to CPR extraction. CPR returns therefore represent the minimum income of the society. Second, households also face different levels of risk on their private projects and allocate thus a share of their labor supply to CPR extraction in order to insure themselves. Whereas Baland and Francois consider separately those two kinds of heterogeneity, the model presented here studies the possible poverty-trap implications of the coexistence of these two roles of the CPR: minimum income and insurance. The main consequence of this extension is that households mix here their labor allocations, while they tend to allocate all their labor to only one activity in Baland and Francois.

2.3.1 *CPR extraction and private project*

As in Baland and Francois (2005), we assume that all labor allocated to the CPR is equivalently productive and receives the average product: $\frac{Y(L) \cdot l_i}{L}$, with $l_i \in [0, 1]$ the amount of labor allocated to the CPR by household i and $L = \int_0^N l_i \, di$ the aggregate amount of labor allocated to the commons.[1] The commons production function, $Y(L)$, is strictly increasing and concave in L. Therefore, the average product is decreasing in L, which constitutes a tragedy-of-the-commons effect: labor allocated by one household has a negative externality on the other households. Moreover, total labor allocated to the commons can be an indicator of environmental damages.

Indeed, the overuse of a resource coincides with the degradation of the ecosystem.

The private projects provide uncertain returns. The expected private project return of household i is $E(\theta_i) \cdot (1 - l_i)$. In the worst case, the private project provides $\underline{\theta_i} \cdot (1 - l_i)$. Note here that only $E(\theta_i)$ and $\underline{\theta_i}$ (and not the whole distribution of the private project returns) are needed to describe the households characteristics. We restrict ourselves to the case of common risk, i.e. we define $\underline{\theta_i} = E(\theta_i) - C$, where C is the same across households. Expected returns, $\overline{E(\theta)}$, and minimum returns, $\underline{\theta}$, constitute a representation of household heterogeneity in terms of skills and risk, respectively.

The households are sorted according to their expected return on the private project. The first household has the lowest expected return and household N has the highest.

2.3.2   Household's objective

At the beginning of the period, each household chooses its labor allocation between the two activities to maximize its expected return $\Pi(l_i)$:

$$\max_{l_i} \ \Pi(l_i) = (1 - l_i) \cdot E(\theta_i) + l_i \cdot \frac{Y(L)}{L} \tag{2.1}$$

Moreover, households need to insure a minimum consumption requirement $C_{\min}$ in the worst state of the world (i.e. if $\underline{\theta_i}$ occurs). We assume here that the minimum requirement is the same across the population. We consider basic needs to survive, such as nutrition. If this requirement is not met, the households decide to migrate. Migration is therefore an outside option for the households if their environment cannot insure their livelihood. We implicitly assume that migration provides the minimum requirement. The choice of any household i to migrate ($M_i = 1$) or not ($M_i = 0$), is therefore

$$\begin{cases} M_i = 1 & \text{if } (1 - l_i) \cdot \underline{\theta_i} + l_i \dfrac{Y(L)}{L} < C_{\min} \\[2mm] M_i = 0 & \text{if } (1 - l_i) \cdot \underline{\theta_i} + l_i \dfrac{Y(L)}{L} \geq C_{\min} \end{cases} \tag{2.2}$$

Thus, households are risk neutral, as long as they get their minimum requirement, and are infinitely risk averse up till that point. We define as poor a household not getting more than its subsistence requirement: it cannot get more from its activities than what it needs to survive. This setup may seem unconventional, but appears quite accurate to describe behaviors of poor communities. Indeed, the main objective of those populations is likely to be insuring survival. Income maximization only comes after this requirement is met.

Two kinds of households decide not to migrate. First, private projects may be profitable enough for some households, even in the worst state of the world: $\underline{\theta_i} \geq C_{min}$. These households are naturally insured. Second, households properly insured by CPR extraction also decide not to migrate. Thus, CPR extraction needs to be profitable enough to insure these households properly, which need to allocate a minimum amount of labor to the CPR. The conditions for these households to stay in the community are as follows:

$$
\begin{cases}
\dfrac{Y(L)}{L} \geq C_{min} \\
\underline{l_i}(L) = \dfrac{C_{min} - \underline{\theta_i}}{\dfrac{Y(L)}{L} - \underline{\theta_i}}
\end{cases}
\tag{2.3}
$$

Return from CPR extraction is decreasing in total labor allocated. Thus, if too much labor is allocated to the CPR, the average product goes down to its bottom value C_{min}. Therefore, a maximum possible amount of labor allocated to the CPR can be defined:

$$
L_{max} : \frac{Y(L_{max})}{L_{max}} = C_{min}
\tag{2.4}
$$

$$
\underline{l_i}(L_{max}) = 1
\tag{2.5}
$$

If too many households are in need of insurance, the insurance capacity of the resource, L_{max}, may be too small. At this point, some households have to migrate and migration occurs until the point at which every remaining household is insured, with the average return being equal to the minimum requirement. Migration is considered here as an action of last resort: the environment cannot provide a livelihood to some households, and thus they have to leave. Households are therefore assumed to migrate from the area if and only if they cannot get their minimum requirement from their livelihood. The number of households having to migrate is therefore

$$
M = \int_0^N M_i \, di = S - L_{max}
\tag{2.6}
$$

with S the population in need of insurance,

$$
S : \underline{\theta_S} = C_{min}
\tag{2.7}
$$

In equilibrium, three classes of households can be distinguished, related to their labor allocation.

2.3.3   *Classes of households at equilibrium*

The equilibrium is a combination of a total amount of labor allocated to the commons, L_e, a share of labor allocated to the commons by each household, l_i, and a number of households that have to migrate, M.

In equilibrium, three classes of households can be distinguished related to their allocation of labor. Two classes are in need of insurance and therefore allocate a share of their labor to CPR extraction, while the third one is "naturally" insured.

UNSKILLED HOUSEHOLDS

Less skilled households have an expected return on the private project less than or equal to the average product on the CPR. These households allocate all their labor to the CPR. Therefore, they get the average product:

$$\text{for } i \in [0; U]: \begin{cases} E(\theta_i) \le \dfrac{Y(L_e)}{L_e} \\[2mm] \theta_i < C_{\min} \\[1mm] l_i = 1 \\[1mm] \Pi(l_i) = \dfrac{Y(L_e)}{L_e} \end{cases} \tag{2.8}$$

CPR extraction is motivated here by a lack of better opportunity. Less skilled households rely on this activity because it requires low-skilled labor and provides higher returns than their private projects.

SKILLED HOUSEHOLDS

Most skilled households are those who get at least their minimum requirement from their private project. Moreover, the expected return on their private project must be greater than the average product on the CPR. Thus, they allocate all their labor to the private project. Their expected income is the expected private return:

$$\text{for } i \in [S; N]: \begin{cases} E(\theta_i) > \dfrac{Y(L_e)}{L_e} \\[2mm] \underline{\theta_i} \ge C_{\min} \\[1mm] l_i = 0 \\[1mm] \Pi(l_i) = E(\theta_i) \end{cases} \tag{2.9}$$

This class of household is naturally insured: they always get enough return from their private project to satisfy their basic needs.

MIDDLE CLASS

This last class of household does not appear in Baland and Francois. For this class, the private project is in expectation more profitable than CPR extraction. However, there are some states of the world in which this private project does not provide their minimum requirement. Therefore, they put some labor into CPR extraction in order to get insured. Because the expected private project return is greater than the return from CPR extraction, these households allocate the minimum amount of labor to the CPR in order to get exactly their minimum requirement in the worst state of the world:

$$
\text{for } i \in [U; S] : \begin{cases} E(\theta_i) > \dfrac{Y(L_e)}{L_e} \\[2mm] \theta_i < C_{\min} \\[2mm] l_i = \underline{l}_i(L_e) \\[2mm] \Pi(l_i) = \underline{l}_i \cdot \dfrac{Y(L_e)}{L_e} + (1 - \underline{l}_i) \cdot E(\theta_i) \end{cases} \tag{2.10}
$$

While in a world with perfect insurance, these middle-class households would allocate all their labor to the private project, they need here to extract from the CPR in order to be properly insured, at the expense of reducing their expected return. Note here that S represents the population in need of insurance (unskilled and middle class). Table 2.1 synthesizes the patterns of the different classes in equilibrium.

Table 2.1 Classes of households in equilibrium

		Unskilled	Middle	Skilled
Households		$[0; U]$	$[U; S]$	$[S; N]$
$E(\theta_i)$		$\leq \dfrac{Y(L_e)}{L_e}$	$> \dfrac{Y(L_e)}{L_e}$	
$\underline{\theta}_i$		$< C_{\min}$		$\geq C_{\min}$
l_i		1	$\underline{l}_i(L_e)$	0
$\Pi(l_i)$		$\dfrac{Y(L_e)}{L_e}$	$\underline{l}_i \cdot \dfrac{Y(L_e)}{L_e} + (1 - \underline{l}_i) \cdot E(\theta_i)$	$E(\theta_i)$

In order to show how CPR extraction becomes a poverty trap, we need to determine the total amount of labor allocated to the CPR.

2.3.4   Equilibrium amount of labor allocated to the CPR

Only two classes of households allocate labor to CPR extraction: unskilled and middle-class households. First, unskilled households allocate all their labor to the CPR. Note here that the number of households classified in the unskilled class depends on the total amount of labor allocated to the CPR:

$$\begin{cases} L_e^U(L_e) = \displaystyle\int_0^{U(L_e)} 1 \, di = U(L_e) \\ U(L_e) : E(\theta_U) = \dfrac{Y(L_e)}{L_e} \end{cases} \tag{2.11}$$

Second, middle-class households allocate only a share of their labor supply to the CPR:

$$\begin{cases} L_e^M(L_e) = \displaystyle\int_{U(L_e)}^S l_i(L_e) \, di \\ S : \underline{\theta}_S = C_{\min} \end{cases} \tag{2.12}$$

The size of the population in need of insurance S is independent of the total amount of labor allocated to the CPR. However, the total amount L_e influences the repartition between unskilled and middle-class households.

CPR extraction constitutes a poverty trap if the average product of CPR extraction goes below the minimum requirement. This situation occurs if too much labor is allocated to the CPR. In this case, CPR extraction cannot properly insure every household in need of insurance, and both unskilled and middle-class households cannot get more than their minimum requirement and allocate all their labor to CPR extraction. They are therefore trapped into poverty because of this over-allocation of labor. Moreover, M households have to migrate until the average return $\frac{Y(L_e)}{L_e}$ equals the minimum requirement $C_{\min}$.

Thus, if CPR extraction does not constitute a poverty trap, the equilibrium amount of labor allocated to the CPR is

$$\begin{cases} L_e = U(L_e) + L_e^M(L_e) \\ \dfrac{Y(L_e)}{L_e} > C_{\min} \\ M = 0 \end{cases} \tag{2.13}$$

Note here that the total amount of labor allocated to the CPR in the non-poverty-trap case is a fixed point which existence needs to be proven (see Appendix 2A).

The equilibrium amount of labor allocated to the CPR in the poverty trap case is

$$\begin{cases} L_e = L_{\max} \\ \dfrac{Y(L_e)}{L_e} = C_{\min} \\ M = S - L_{\max} \end{cases} \tag{2.14}$$

At this point, it is possible to describe the two types of situation.

2.4 Tragedy of the commons and poverty trap

It is well known that an open-access resource suffers from the tragedy of the commons: individuals do not take into account the negative externality of their actions on the others. In the case studied here, with CPR used as insurance and minimum income, this phenomenon can lead to a poverty trap: the population in need of insurance (unskilled and middle class households) is trapped in CPR extraction and cannot get more than its minimum requirement. Moreover, some households have to migrate.

2.4.1 Insurance without poverty trap

We consider here the case where $L_e < L_{\max}$. Therefore, the insurance use of the CPR does not lead to a poverty trap. Nevertheless, CPR extraction is characterized by a tragedy-of-the-commons process. Note, for example, that both unskilled and middle-class households would be better off with an insurance scheme. Indeed, middle-class households could allocate all their labor to their private project, which is more profitable in expectation. Moreover, the unskilled households would be better off too, because the labor supply allocated to the commons and thus the tragedy-of-the-commons effect would be lower. Therefore, the average product of CPR extraction would be bigger. Figure 2.1 illustrates this case.

2.4.2 Insurance with poverty trap

The poverty-trap case is a result of $L_e = L_{\max}$, $M > 0$. More precisely, it is essentially an extreme consequence of the tragedy of the commons described before. As already shown, M households have to migrate until the point at which the average product of CPR extraction reach the minimum requirement. At this point, middle-class households have to allocate

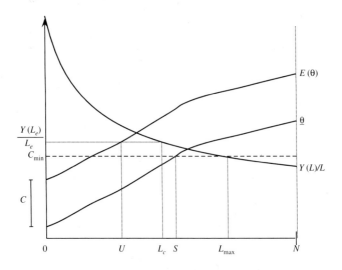

Figure 2.1 Insurance with no poverty trap and common risk.

all their labor to the CPR in order to be insured. Therefore, both unskilled and middle-class households are perfectly insured but cannot get more than their minimum requirement, which constitutes a poverty trap (as defined in introduction). Figure 2.2 describes the poverty-trap case. Note here that skilled households get the same outcome whatever the type of situation.

2.4.3   The causes of the poverty trap

A poverty trap is therefore the result of two main factors. First, population factors are important. If the population in need of insurance (S) is large, the poverty-trap case is more likely. The size of this population is a consequence of two components: distribution of skills ($E(\theta)$) and distribution of risk ($\underline{\theta}$). First, the larger the population with relatively high expected return on the private profit, the smaller the unskilled population. Second, the smaller the risk at which the households are exposed, the larger the population that does not depend on the resource.

Second, the CPR extraction function determines the threshold of population (L_{max}) able to exploit it. If the environment is fragile, it is quickly saturated and the threshold is low.

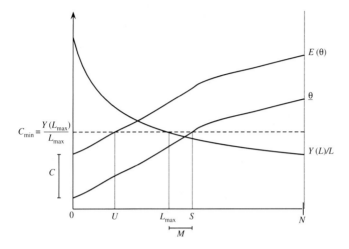

Figure 2.2 Insurance with poverty trap and common risk.

PROPOSITION 2.1 *In a context of risk on the private projects, the use of CPR extraction as insurance and minimum income can lead to a poverty trap if the population in need of insurance is too large and the resource has low capacity. Then, both unskilled and middle-class households are trapped in CPR extraction and cannot get more than their basic needs in return.*

Proof: A poverty-trap situation is characterized by $L_e = L_{max}$, $\Pi(l_i) = C_{min}$ and $l_i = 1$ for households $[O; L_{max}]$, and $M = S - L_{max}$. S determines the equilibrium amount of labor allocated to the CPR (L_e), while the capacity of the resource determines the production function, and thus the maximum amount of labor allocated to the CPR (L_{max}).   □

As already mentioned, the poverty-trap situation is an extreme case of a tragedy of the commons. The only difference in terms of welfare between those two cases is the fact that the middle class *de facto* disappears when CPR extraction becomes a poverty trap. Indeed, middle-class households can be insured only at the cost of allocating all their labor to the CPR. They lose therefore all the extra return they could get from their private project. Only two classes of households remain in the society: unskilled and skilled households.

The case studied here therefore has implications in terms of both development and environment. At the same time, the population using the resource is trapped in poverty, and the resource they use is over-exploited.

However, another equilibrium may be sustainable at the same time, if a cooperative shift of labor allocation is made by middle-class households.

2.5 Inter-households insurance

Allowing for inter-household insurance may allow for a cooperative equilibrium outside the poverty trap. Indeed, a cooperative shift in the labor allocation may provide an equilibrium in which every household is insured and the minimum income is above the minimum requirement.

Indeed, consider the following insurance contract.[2] Middle-class households commit not to allocate any labor to the CPR, which would raise the return to CPR extraction above the minimum requirement: $\frac{Y(U^c)}{U^c} \geq C_{min}$. Conversely, if middle-class households get poor return from their private project ($\theta < C_{min}$), unskilled households commit to compensate for it, filling the gap between the private outputs and the minimum requirement: $C_{min} - \theta$. Thus, middle-class households could concentrate on the most profitable activity, being insured to get at least their minimum requirement. Moreover, unskilled households would get more than their minimum requirement, since labor allocated to the CPR would be reduced.

The number of unskilled households in this cooperative equilibrium would be larger than in the preceding one, but they would be the only households to allocate labor to CPR extraction. Moreover, as these households allocate all their labor to the CPR, the number of unskilled households is also the equilibrium labor allocation to the CPR: $L_c = U^c$. The unskilled class would be defined as follows:

$$for \ i \in [0; U^c]: \begin{cases} E(\theta_i) \leq \dfrac{Y(U^c)}{U^c} \\ \underline{\theta_i} < C_{min} \\ l_i = 1 \end{cases} \tag{2.15}$$

Middle-class households would now allocate all their labor to their private project, which is more profitable in expectation:

$$for \ i \in [U^c; S]: \begin{cases} E(\theta_i) > \dfrac{Y(U^c)}{U^c} \\ \underline{\theta_i} < C_{min} \\ l_i = 0 \end{cases} \tag{2.16}$$

Table 2.2 Classes of households with inter-household insurance

	Unskilled	Middle	Skilled
Households	$[0; U^c]$	$[U^c; S]$	$[S; N]$
$E(\theta_i)$	$\leq \dfrac{Y(U^c)}{U^c}$		$> \dfrac{Y(U^c)}{U^c}$
$\underline{\theta}_i$	$< C_{min}$		$\geq C_{min}$
l_i	1		0

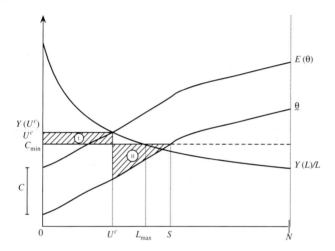

Figure 2.3 Inter-household insurance.

Finally, the skilled class would remain unchanged:

$$for\ i \in [S; N]: \begin{cases} E(\theta_i) > \dfrac{Y(U^c)}{U^c} \\ \underline{\theta}_i \geq C_{min} \\ l_i = 0 \end{cases} \qquad (2.17)$$

Table 2.2 shows these equilibrium classes.

This new equilibrium, represented in Figure 2.3, could be sustained as long as the total increase in CPR extraction could compensate every middle-class household if the worst state of the world occurs:

$$U^c \left(\frac{Y(U^c)}{U^c} - C_{min} \right) \geq \int_{U^e}^{S} (C_{min} - \underline{\theta}_i)\, di \qquad (2.18)$$

Graphically, equation (2.18) holds if zone I is larger than or equal to zone II in Figure 2.3.

Basically this cooperative equilibrium consists of unskilled households insuring middle-class households for the risk they take. Unskilled households would not be directly compensated for providing insurance, but they may have an interest in subsidizing insurance because it would increase their return from CPR extraction. This is therefore a win–win opportunity for both types of households.

The cooperative insurance capacity (zone I of Figure 2.3) represents the maximum amount available to compensate middle-class households. Its size depends mainly on the capacity of the resource and especially the CPR extraction function. If the average return to CPR extraction decreases quickly, a reduction in labor allocated can have an important effect on the size of zone I. Figure 2.4 shows the impact of the CPR extraction function on the cooperative insurance capacity. Return from CPR extraction decreases more quickly in the left graph, while both functions have the same maximum capacity L_{max}. Potential efficiency gains are thus more important in the left graph, which reveals a better cooperative insurance capacity.

The cooperative insurance needs are represented in zone II and consist of the amount that is necessary to properly insure every middle-class household if the worst state of the world occurs. Its size depends on aggregate risk. If a lot of middle-class households have the very low, worst possible output, the decrease in labor allocated may be insufficient to properly insure every households. Figure 2.5 shows the impact of risk on the cooperative insurance needs. Aggregate risk is more important in the lower graph, which creates larger insurance needs than in the upper graph.

Thus, if some conditions are met concerning the distribution of risk and the extraction function of the common resource, an inter-household

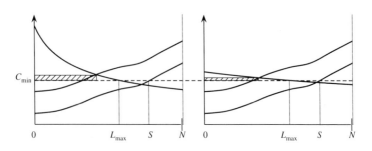

Figure 2.4 The cooperative insurance capacity increases with the slope of the CPR extraction function.

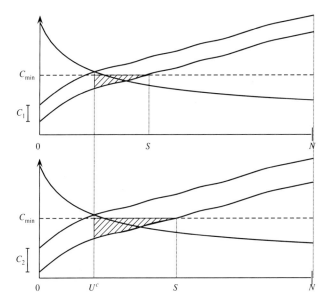

Figure 2.5 Stronger aggregate risk ($C_1 < C_2$) increases the cooperative insurance needs.

insurance scheme may provide a cooperative equilibrium outside the poverty trap. If the condition described in equation (2.18) is not respected, however, this type of equilibrium cannot be sustained. In this case, a private insurance mechanism may offer another type of solution.

2.6   Private insurance mechanism

Another potential solution to the poverty trap described above could be the introduction of a private insurance mechanism. In the setup presented here, an insurance scheme would consist of paying a risk premium in order to get the minimum requirement in case of economic stress. The insurance system would therefore be paid a premium p_i by insured households and would fill the gap between a bad private return and the consumption requirement (i.e. $C_{min} - \theta_i$ if the worst state of the world occurs).

The risk premium therefore depends on the amount the insurance system would have to pay to fill the gap between the worst private outcome and the minimum requirement. Less skilled households would therefore have to pay a higher risk premium: $\frac{\partial p_i}{\partial \theta_i} < 0$. Moreover, this risk premium would be increasing in the probability of occurrence of bad states of the world.

First, skilled households would not be interested in this insurance scheme, because they are naturally insured. Therefore, only households belonging to classes in need of insurance (S) could be willing to subscribe. Second, less skilled households, with too high risk premiums, could not afford the insurance scheme, and would not subscribe. Thus, only some middle-class households subscribe to the insurance.

The condition for subscribing to the insurance is:

$$E(\theta_i) - p_i \geq (1 - \underline{l_i}) \cdot E(\theta_i) + \underline{l_i} \cdot \frac{Y(L_s)}{L_s} \tag{2.19}$$

which implies that household i subscribes to the insurance if the risk premium is not to high. L_s is the new equilibrium amount of labor allocated to the CPR.

Two types of middle-class households can now be distinguished. Some of them subscribe to the insurance,

$$for \ i \in [S^s; S]: \begin{cases} p_i \leq \underline{l_i} \cdot \left(E(\theta_i) - \dfrac{Y(L_s)}{L_s} \right) \\ \underline{\theta_i} < C_{\min} \\ l_i = 0 \end{cases} \tag{2.20}$$

while other middle-class households keep on using CPR extraction as insurance, because the insurance scheme is too expensive for them,

$$for \ i \in [U^s; S^s]: \begin{cases} p_i > \underline{l_i} \cdot \left(E(\theta_i) - \dfrac{Y(L_s)}{L_s} \right) \\ \underline{\theta_i} < C_{\min} \\ l_i = \underline{l_i}(L_s) \end{cases} \tag{2.21}$$

Here S^s is the first household subscribing to the insurance scheme and U^s is the first middle-class household. Table 2.3 describes the new classes in equilibrium.

The new equilibrium amount of labor allocated to the CPR is

$$\begin{cases} L_s = U^s(L_s) + \displaystyle\int_{U^s(L_s)}^{S^s} \underline{l_i}(L_s) \, di \\ U^s(L_s) : E(\theta_{U^s}) = \dfrac{Y(L_s)}{L_s} \\ S^s(p) : p_{S^s} = \underline{l_{S^s}} \cdot \left(E(\theta_{S^s}) - \dfrac{Y(L_s)}{L_s} \right) \end{cases} \tag{2.22}$$

Table 2.3 Classes of households with private insurance

	Unskilled	Middle without insurance	Middle without insurance	Skilled
Households	$[0; U^s]$	$[U^s; S^s]$	$[S^s; S]$	$[S; N]$
$E(\theta_i)$	$\leq \dfrac{Y(L_s)}{L_s}$	$> \dfrac{Y(L_s)}{L_s}$		
p_i	$> \underline{l_i} \cdot (E(\theta_i) - \dfrac{Y(L_s)}{L_s})$		$\leq \underline{l_i} \cdot (E(\theta_i) - \dfrac{Y(L_s)}{L_s})$	
$\underline{\theta_i}$		$< C_{min}$		$\geq C_{min}$
l_i	1	$\underline{l_i}(L_s)$	0	

Several implications of the introduction of an insurance scheme can be determined. First, the population in need of insurance S remains stable, because the conditions for being in the skilled class do not change. Second, if some households subscribe to the insurance scheme, the population allocating labor to the CPR decreases, $S^s < S$, and total labor allocated to CPR extraction decreases, $L_s < L_e$. Third, since the equilibrium amount of labor allocated to the resource decreases, average return from CPR extraction increases. Therefore, the amount of labor allocated by middle-class households not subscribing to the insurance decreases, because less labor is needed to fill the gap between the worst private outcome and the minimum requirement: $l_i(L_s) < l_i(L_e)$. Finally, the number of unskilled households increases, $U^s > U$, and their welfare increases, $\dfrac{Y(L_s)}{L_s} > \dfrac{Y(L_e)}{L_e}$.

Overall, the introduction of a private insurance scheme may be a solution to the poverty trap case described above, if the number of subscribing households is sufficiently large, thus if the risk premiums are not too high, and the middle class sufficiently important.

2.7 Conclusion

The aim of this chapter is to show how a CPR used as insurance may become a poverty trap. Namely, this mechanism can be described as an extreme case of a tragedy of the commons.

We consider here a CPR used as insurance and which provides a minimum level of income to the society. If the resource has low capacity, i.e. if its exploitation is quickly saturated, the poverty trap is more likely. Moreover, if the population in need of insurance is too large, this use of the resource is also more likely to lead to a poverty trap. If the first condition is not under the control of anything but nature, the second one has some implications in terms of economic and social polices.

If some conditions on the extraction function and the population distribution are met, the development of cooperative insurance mechanisms may reduce labor allocated to CPR extraction enough to sustain other equilibria outside the poverty trap. Moreover, private insurance schemes may also be potential solutions to the poverty trap. In this context, reducing risk may be a useful tool to attain both objectives of development and protection of natural resources.

Educational policies should also have an impact in term of skills. Indeed, a more educated population leads to a smaller population in need of the resource to obtain a minimum income. The introduction of a minimum income by the welfare state could also reduce the minimum income use of the resource.

Finally, an important restriction here is that the size of the resource is supposed to be fixed. If some policies reduce the dependence of the populations to the resource, a possible consequence is the decrease in the size of the resource, because of a decrease in its perceived value (see Chapter 1 above).

Overall, even if the literature gives the insight that CPRs have important insurance properties, very few empirical analysis and case studies consider how the introduction of insurance mechanisms and microcredit affects the use of common property resources. Chapter 1 above considers the extensive land use and advances the idea that introducing insurance may decrease the forest cover. In contrast, focusing on intensive labor allocation, this chapter argues that the introduction of inter-household or private insurance may release pressure on common forests and decrease poverty at the same time. Some empirical analysis and case studies would thus be required to give some evidence of those two effects and to distinguish which one is the most important.

Appendix 2A: L_e as a fixed point

The total amount of labor allocated to the CPR in the non-poverty-trap case is a fixed point. First, we need to prove that $U(L_e) + L_e^M(L_e)$ is decreasing in L_e.

Note that $U(L_e)$ is decreasing in L_e. Indeed, the number of unskilled people is defined as $E(\theta_U) \leq Y(L_e)/L_e$, which is decreasing in L_e by assumption.

Therefore, if L_e increases, some households pass from the unskilled class to the middle class. Those households reduce the amount of labor allocated to the CPR. Indeed, the unskilled households allocate all their labor to the CPR, while middle-class households allocate only a share of it.

Overall, an increase in L_e induces a reduction in labor allocated by the unskilled class, which over-compensate the raise in labor allocated by the middle-class households. It follows that the total amount of labor allocated to the CPR decreases.

Second, $U(L_e) + L_e^M(L_e)$ is positive, as the amount of labor allocated by insurance-seeking households is necessarily positive. It follows that $L_e = U(L_e) + L_e^M(L_e)$ is a fixed point.

References

Agarwal, B. (1991) Social security and the family: coping with seasonality and calamity in rural India. In E. J. Ahmad, J. Dreze, J. Hills, and A. Sen (eds), *Social Security in Developing Countries*. Oxford: Clarendon Press, pp. 171–244.

Anderson, C., Locker, L. and Nugent R. (2002) Microcredit, social capital, and common pool resources. *World Development*, 30(1): 95–105.

Angelsen, A., Sunderlin, W., Ahmad Dermawan, D. and Rianto, E. (2001) Economic crisis, small farmer well-being, and forest cover change in Indonesia. *World Development*, 29(5).

Angelsen, A. and Wunder, S. (2002) Exploring the forest-poverty link. CIFOR Occasional Paper no. 40.

Azariadis, C. and Stachurski, J. (2005) Poverty traps. In P. Aghion and S. Durlauf (eds), *Handbook of Economic Growth*. Elsevier, pp. 295–384.

Baland, J. and Francois, P. (2005) Commons as insurance and the welfare impact of privatization. *Journal of Public Economics*, 89(2–3): 211–231.

Bromley, D. and Chavas, J. (1989) On risk, transactions and economic development in the semiarid tropics. *Economic Development and Cultural Change*, 37: 719–36.

Dasgupta, M. (1987) Informal security mechanisms and population retention in rural India. *Economic Development and Cultural Change*, 36(1): 101–20.

Dasgupta, P. and Mäler, K.-G. (1993) Poverty, institutions and the environmental resource base. In J. Behrman and T.N. Srinavasan (eds), *Handbook of Development Economics*, Vol. 3. Amsterdam: North-Holland.

Godoy, R., O'Neill, K., Groff, S., Kostishack, P., Cubas, A., Demmer, J., McSweeney, K., Overman, J., Wilkie, D., Brokaw, N. and Martinez, M. (1997) Household determinants of deforestation by Amerindians in Honduras, *World Development*, 25(6): 977– 987.

Jodha, N. (1986) Common property resources and rural poor in dry regions of India. *Economic and Political Weekly*, 21(27): 1169–81.

McSweeney, K. (2003) Tropical forests as safety nets? the relative importance of forest product sale as smallholder insurance, Eastern Honduras. *Society and Natural Resources*, 17(1): 39–56.

McSweeney, K. (2005) Natural insurance, forest access, and compounded misfortune: forest re-sources in smallholder coping strategies before and after Hurricane Mitch, Northeastern Honduras. *World Development*, 33(9): 1453–71.

Neumann, R. and Hirsch, E. (2000) Commercialisation of non-timber forest products: a review. Technical report, CIFOR, Bogor, Indonesia and FAO, Rome.

Pattanayak, S. and Sills, E. (2001) Do tropical forests provide natural insurance? The microeconomics of non-timber forest product collection in the Brazilian Amazon. *Land Economics*, 77(4): 595–612.

Reddy, S. and Chakravaty, S. (1999) Forest dependence and income distribution in a subsistence economy. *World Development*, 27(7): 1141–9.

Wunder, S. (2001) Poverty alleviation and tropical forests: What scope for synergies? *World Development*, 29: 1817–33.

Part III

National

Forest management, corruption and illegal logging

3 How size of concessions may influence systemic corruption in forest harvesting

A theoretical assessment

3.1 Introduction

Corruption, i.e. "the unlawful use of public office for private gain" (Transparency International 2003), is one of the main underlying causes of deforestation and over-harvesting of natural resources (Amacher 2006). Illegal logging represents more than 90 percent of logging in Indonesia (Dudley *et al.* 1995), 80 percent in Brazil and 90 percent in Cambodia (Winbourne 2002). In Indonesia, logging concessions covering more than half the country's total forest area were awarded by former President Suharto, many of them to his relatives and political allies (Global Forest Watch, World Resource Institute). In 1995, in Cambodia, the two prime ministers in power at that time gave concessions, contrary to the law, for the remaining parts of tropical forest (Harris White 1996).[1]

Addressing this issue of corruption and forest harvesting requires us to define the type of corruption considered. An important distinction is between policy-maker and bureaucratic corruption (Rose-Ackerman 1978, 1999; World Bank 2000; Wilson and Damania 2005). First, policy-maker or "grand" corruption consists of offering bribes to the policy-maker in order to influence his policy choices. Second, bureaucratic or "petty" corruption consists of paying bribes to civil agents to avoid the consequences of a particular rule. Of course, the two types of corruption are rarely observed separately. Corruption is generally a systemic phenomenon. A corrupt policy-maker often coexists with a corrupt bureaucracy, and modification vice versa. Moreover, both kinds of corruption may interact. A key objective of this chapter is thus to analyze how bureaucratic corruption may be linked to policy-maker corruption in the context of forest harvesting.

An important pattern of forest management is the allocation of forest concessions to logging firms. The policy-maker is supposed to decide both the size of the forest to exploit, the number of loggers harvesting it (or number of concessions) and thus the size of concessions. Case studies usually notice the large variety of forest policies (see Karsenty 2007, for Central and West Africa). An increased knowledge of the links between systemic corruption, over-harvesting of forest resources and forest policies is thus a crucial issue. In this context, it appears that the size of concessions plays a key role in determining those relationships.

The first part of this chapter investigates the impact of concession size and bureaucratic corruption on forest over-harvesting, taking the forest policy as given. The logging firms may be inspected by a bureaucrat they might be willing to bribe. An uncorrupt authority may audit both the firm and the bureaucrat to verify the enforcement of the forest policy. Two factors influence the impact of bureaucratic corruption. First, a large number of loggers reduces the probability of the firm being inspected by the bureaucrat and audited by the authority. Therefore, a large number of loggers decreases the expected penalty and is an incentive not to respect the logging rules and to over-harvest the forest resources. Second, the size of concessions is important through its impact on marginal productivity of effort. Considering previous studies, it is difficult to have a clear idea of the impact of the size of concessions on the productivity of effort. Thus, both cases of positive and negative impact have to be considered. If the marginal productivity of effort decreases with the size of concessions, small concessions represent an incentive to over-harvest the forest. In this case, a larger number of concessions tends to increase forest over-harvesting. Moreover, a larger harvested forest area and more stringent harvest quota tend to decrease logging intensity and over-harvesting.

The second part presents a model of policy-maker corruption, following Grossman and Helpman (1994). The policy-maker designs the forest policy, which consists of the number of concessions, the size of the forest to be harvested and the maximum harvest intensity. It maximizes a weighted sum of social welfare and received bribes. An exogenous number of firms act as one lobby, bribing the policy-maker to set a more permissive forest policy, i.e. to increase the size of the harvested forest, the number of concessions and the harvest quota. In this context, the policy-maker tends to set a suboptimal and overly permissive forest policy, when more corrupt.

Considering the links between policy-maker and bureaucratic corruption, this chapter supports partially the idea of systemic corruption. Indeed, policy-maker corruption tends to enhance the impact of bureaucratic corruption through two key policy instruments, and to decrease it through a third. The net impact remains to be determined, but depends crucially on the specification of the loggers' net harvest function, of the welfare function and of the bribe schedule.

Section 3.2 presents a short literature review on the links between corruption and forest harvesting. Bureaucratic corruption is analyzed in Section 3.3, while Section 3.4 presents a model of policy-maker corruption.

Finally, Section 3.5 discusses the systemic patterns of the models presented and Section 3.6 concludes and discusses the policy implications.

3.2 Corruption and the environment

Some papers consider the impact of corruption (or lobbying) on forest harvesting. Using a political economy model, Eerola (2004) considers two lobbies, the timber industry and an environmental organization, competing to influence a government choice. The timber industry is a monopoly and the policy instrument is the level of conservation of the country's forests. One of the main results of the paper is that an exporting monopoly tends to face stricter conservation policies than a monopoly producing for the domestic market, because the costs of conservation are partly borne by foreign consumers when the timber is exported.

The context described by Eerola may not fit with the context of many developing countries. First, the political influence of environmental organizations in developing countries is often weak compared to that of the logging industry. Considering competition between both types of actors is likely not to be relevant in the case we analyze here. Second, even if forestry sectors are usually quite concentrated, assuming a monopoly restricts the analysis too much, avoiding potential interactions between logging firms. Third, Eerola assumes that forest harvesting provides constant a return to scale. In contrast, this chapter states that the influence of the size of concessions on the marginal productivity of effort may be of importance in determining returns to effort and thus incentive to over-harvest. Finally, it is assumed that two uses of timber may be considered: roundwood and the production of a wood product. However, most developing countries have weak opportunities to transform the timber locally, and have only the opportunity to sale non-transformed timber. Overall, it seems that the context described by Eerola fits the situation of industrialized countries better than that of developing countries.

Barbier *et al.* (2005) consider and test the influence of terms of trade, resource dependency, and corruption on resource conversion. Their main finding is that increased corruption and resource dependency and decreasing terms of trade increase land conversion.

These two papers consider land conversion (or forest conservation) as the unique instrument of the forest policy. In contrast, we consider a policy mix, including an indicator of land conversion (size of the harvested forest), a quota on forest exploitation (maximum harvest effort), and an indicator of forestry sector concentration (number of concessions). This extension thus gives an overview of the complexity of the forest policy, by considering both the extensive and the intensive side of forest degradation.

Amacher *et al.* (2008) also consider the design of the forest policy as a mix between several instruments. They analyze how bureaucratic corruption may influence the policy design by an uncorrupt government. In their paper, the authors consider that the policy-maker may anticipate corruption, and take its occurrence into consideration when choosing the forest policy. In contrast, we consider that both bureaucrats and the policy-maker may be corrupt, and that both types of corruption may be interrelated.

Indeed, the three papers mentioned above only analyze one type of corruption: government corruption in the case of Eerola and Barbier *et al.* and bureaucratic corruption in the case of Amacher *et al.* However, as mentioned above, corruption is often systemic, and distinguishing policy-maker and bureaucratic corruption is important and relevant when analyzing developing world contexts. To our knowledge, Wilson and Damania (2005) were first to consider this two-scale corruption. The authors show that political competition increases the stringency of the environmental policy, but that its impact is limited. Indeed, if judicial institutions are weak, an increase in political competition may increase bureaucratic corruption, which limits the enforcement of the environmental policy. Moreover, political competition does not necessarily deter bureaucratic corruption.

Although Wilson and Damania (2005) consider pollution in an industrialized country, their two-step analysis is relevant to the analysis of the systemic patterns of corruption in developing countries. Thus, we consider it in the context of developing countries to study the occurrence of corruption at different government levels and its effects on forest harvesting. The object of this study is, however, quite different. Wilson and Damania focus their analysis on the links between corruption and political competition, and their impact on environmental policies. In contrast, we study an incumbent government and focus our analysis on the importance of scale effects on systemic corruption and forest policy design.

Proceeding backward, in the next section we will analyze bureaucratic corruption, considering the forest policy as given. Then we will consider the forest policy choice process.

3.3   The size of concessions and bureaucratic corruption

The forest policy is assumed to have been designed by the policy-maker. It consists of the size of the forest to be harvested $\overline{F}$, the number of concessions, $\overline{N}$, and the maximum harvest effort, $\bar{e}$. This last policy instrument can be considered as a harvest quota.[2] For example, it can be the minimum rotation age, or a maximum amount of timber to log per hectare. We proceed backward. $\overline{F}$, $\overline{N}$ and $\bar{e}$ are considered as given by the firm. In the next section, the forest policy choice process is described.

We assume that the logging firms have an interest in not respecting the quota and in setting $e > \bar{e}$, i.e. a positive level of non-compliance $v = e - \bar{e} > 0$. To verify that the quota is respected, bureaucrats may inspect the logging firm. However, the means being limited, only a fixed number of loggers N^c can be inspected. Moreover, if the inspected firm does not respect the effort limit, it may offer a bribe B to the bureaucrat, in order for him to declare that the quota has been respected.

Finally, an independent uncorrupt authority is in charge of auditing both the bureaucrat and the firm, to verify the enforcement of the forest policy. If both parties are convicted of over-harvesting and corruption, the authority imposes some penalties per hectare (proportional to the level of non-compliance), $h^f(v)$ and $h^b(v)$, on the firm and the bureaucrat, respectively. The authority audits a share σ of the inspected loggers.[3] Assuming such an authority allows different cases of anti-corruption policies to be considered. At one extreme, the authority has no means to audit loggers: $\sigma = 0$. At the other extreme, the authority has full means to fight against corruption, and audit every inspected firm: $\sigma = 1$. The control potential of such an authority depends on the countries' institutions. The existence of an independent authority may come from international organizations. For instance, anti-corruption policies are one of the main objective behind World Bank interventions.

3.3.1 The logger–bureaucrat interaction

The logger

The size of concessions is the result of the forest policy chosen by the government: $\bar{N}$ concessions of size $s = \frac{\bar{F}}{\bar{N}}$.

Harvest and land-holding costs and timber prices are integrated in the net harvest function. Loggers are price takers, which makes sense if we consider a small open economy: harvesting firms trade at the international market price and do not influence this price. In this sense, concentration is addressed through the impact of the number of logging firms and the size of concessions on corruption.

The net harvest function depends on the size of concessions (exogenous to the logger) and the logging effort (the logger's choice variable), and takes the form $H(s; e)$, with standard properties $H_e > 0$, $H_{ee} < 0$, $H_s > 0$, $H_{ss} < 0$.[4] The number of loggers and the size of the harvested forest determine the size of concessions, which implies that $H(s; e) = H(\frac{\bar{F}}{N}, e)$, $H_F = \frac{H_s}{N} > 0$, $H_N = \frac{-F H_s}{N^2} < 0$, $H_{FF} = \frac{H_{ss}}{N^2} < 0$, and $H_{NN} = \frac{F}{N^4}(H_{ss} - 2N H^s) < 0$.

THE IMPACT OF THE SIZE OF CONCESSIONS ON EFFORT PRODUCTIVITY

This is represented by the effect of the size of concessions on the net marginal productivity of effort (H_{se}).

Forest harvesting involves potentially important costs of implementation. It seems plausible that transport costs and the costs of opening access (mainly the creation of roads) to the forest are positively correlated with the size of concessions, which tend to decrease the net marginal productivity of effort. Moreover, loggers may cooperate and share a part of opening access costs, which suggests that the size of concessions decreases the net marginal productivity of effort. On the other hand, small concessions may generate congestion and thus decrease the marginal productivity of effort.

Intuitively, countries with a relatively long history of forest harvesting are likely to experience smaller implementation costs, due to existing infrastructures and learning by doing. Conversely, countries with less accessible forests (e.g. in mountain regions) probably have larger transport and road creation costs. Therefore, this relationship is potentially highly dependent on the country considered.

Only few studies treat this issue. Ruiz Perez *et al.* (2005) find a negative relationship between the size of concessions and logging ratio (i.e. the surface area of the concessions that is logged) in the Congo Basin. This suggests a higher pressure on small concessions (and thus $H_{se} < 0$). Gray (2002) also describes small concessions as an incentive for unsustainable logging. Finally, Gray (2000) argues that "large concessions . . . have little incentive . . . to practice more intensive forest management", which also suggests that marginal productivity of logging effort decreases with the size of concessions.

Although those case studies tend to validate the hypothesis of decreasing returns with the size of concessions, empirical evidence is rather meagre. It is therefore difficult to conclude the links between the effort net marginal productivity and the size of concessions. We will thus consider all cases in this chapter, keeping in mind that this relationship may go both ways.

The loggers may have an interest in exceeding the harvest quota imposed by the policy-maker: $H(\frac{\bar{F}}{N}; \bar{e}) < H(\frac{\bar{F}}{N}; e^*)$, with $\bar{e} < e^*$. As an extreme case, both players have the same optimum, $e^* = \bar{e}$, and the problem is trivial. Indeed, an inter-temporal profit maximization would suggest that a logger would not over-exploit the resource because of expected future losses. Unsustainable forest exploitation is nevertheless frequently observed. First, short-term concessions and/or political instability may be a source of incentive to exceed the logging limits. If the logger anticipates that he may lose his concession in the next period, he is likely not to respect sustainability. Second, non-internalization of externalities could represent an incentive not to respect the logging limits: if environmental damages of over-harvesting are borne by other agents than loggers (local communities, biodiversity losses, etc.), it may be profitable for them to exceed the logging quotas.

In this chapter, we take these incentives as given and focus the analysis on their consequences.

The logger may be inspected with probability $\frac{N^c}{N}$. Thus, a larger number of loggers decreases the individual probability of being inspected. One could argue that the number of inspected loggers should depend on the size of concessions. Indeed, a logger with a large concession could take longer to inspect that a logger with a smaller concession. Thus, N^c would be positively related to $\overline{N}$, which decreases the size of concessions: $\frac{\partial N^c}{\partial s} < 0$, $\frac{\partial N^c}{\partial \overline{N}} > 0$. Such an assumption would reduce this dilution effect, and mitigate the following results. Nevertheless, those results would still hold if $\frac{\partial N^c}{\partial \overline{N}} < \frac{N^c}{\overline{N}}$. We thus keep a fixed N^c, not depending on $\overline{N}$.

The logger possibly pays the bureaucrat a bribe B. In this case, with probability $\sigma \frac{N^c}{N}$, the authority audits and the logger has to pay a penalty $\frac{\overline{F}}{N} h^f(v)$. Note that the penalty is increasing and convex in the level of non-compliance v: $\partial h^i / \partial v > 0$ and $\partial^2 h^i / \partial v^2 > 0$, for $i = f, b$. It is also proportional to the size of concessions $\frac{\overline{F}}{N}$.

Overall, the logger has to make two choices. First, it chooses whether to respect the quota (set $e = \bar{e}$) or not. Second, if the logger has chosen to cheat and is inspected, it has to choose whether to bribe the bureaucrat (and set $e^* > \bar{e}$) or to accept to pay the fine (and set $e^{**} > \bar{e}$). If choosing to pay a bribe, the logger still risks being audited by the independent authority (with probability σ) and having to pay the fine anyway. The following table summarizes the different strategies and payoffs.

	Not inspected	Inspected Not audited	Inspected by the bureaucrat Audited by the authority
Probability	$1 - \dfrac{N^c}{N}$	$(1-\sigma)\dfrac{N^c}{N}$	$\sigma\dfrac{N^c}{N}$
Respect	$H\left(\dfrac{\overline{F}}{N}; \bar{e}\right)$	$H\left(\dfrac{\overline{F}}{N}; \bar{e}\right)$	$H\left(\dfrac{\overline{F}}{N}; \bar{e}\right)$
Cheat/pay the fine	$H\left(\dfrac{\overline{F}}{N}; e^{**}\right)$	$H\left(\dfrac{\overline{F}}{N}; e^{**}\right)$ $-\dfrac{\overline{F}}{N} h^f(e^{**} - \bar{e})$	$H\left(\dfrac{\overline{F}}{N}; e^{**}\right)$ $-\dfrac{\overline{F}}{N} h^f(e^{**} - \bar{e})$
Cheat/bribe	$H\left(\dfrac{\overline{F}}{N}; e^*\right)$	$H\left(\dfrac{\overline{F}}{N}; e^*\right) - B$	$H\left(\dfrac{\overline{F}}{N}; e^*\right)$ $-\left[B + \dfrac{\overline{F}}{N} h^f(e^* - \bar{e})\right]$

Consequently the strategies and their related expected payoffs are presented in the following diagram.

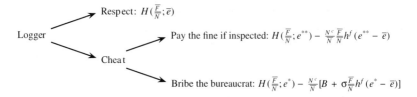

The purpose of the fine is to enforce the harvest quota and therefore deter incentives to cheat. Thus, it seems reasonable to assume that the fine is set such that the *cheat/pay-the-fine* strategy is dominated by the *respect* strategy, which implies that the expected fine should exceed the harvest gains from cheating:

$$\frac{N^c}{N}\frac{\overline{F}}{N}h^f(e^{**}-\bar{e}) > H\left(\frac{\overline{F}}{N};e^{**}\right) - H\left(\frac{\overline{F}}{N};\bar{e}\right) \qquad (3.1)$$

Moreover, the *cheat/bribe* strategy is strictly dominant if

$$B < \frac{N}{N^c}\left(H\left(\frac{\overline{F}}{N};e^{*}\right) - H\left(\frac{\overline{F}}{N};\bar{e}\right)\right) - \sigma\frac{\overline{F}}{N}h^f(e^{*}-\bar{e}) \equiv \bar{B} \qquad (3.2)$$

The *cheat/bribe* strategy is chosen if the expected bribe is cheap enough to compensate for the potential fine involved by the audit. $\bar{B}$ therefore represents the reservation value of the bribe for the logger.

The logger's expected net benefit from the bribe is the expected payoff from the *cheat/bribe* strategy, minus the payoff of the *respect* strategy, i.e. the safe strategy:

$$\Psi^f = H\left(\frac{\overline{F}}{N};e\right) - \frac{N^c}{N}\left[B + \sigma\frac{\overline{F}}{N}h^f(v)\right] - H\left(\frac{\overline{F}}{N};\bar{e}\right) \qquad (3.3)$$

When choosing the *cheat/bribe* strategy, the logger gets a larger net output $H(\frac{\overline{F}}{N};e)$. It is inspected by the bureaucrat with probability $\frac{N^c}{N}$ and pays a bribe B. Moreover, it may be convicted by the audit authority with probability $\frac{N^c}{N}\sigma$ and pay a fine $\frac{\overline{F}}{N}h^f(v)$. Finally, the *respect* strategy provides a safe payoff $H(\frac{\overline{F}}{N};\bar{e})$.

The bureaucrat

The bureaucrat is risk-neutral and gets a wage w for each inspected logger. Assuming the inspected logger did not respect the harvest quota and offers a bribe, he may accept the offer and be audited with probability σ. If he is convicted, he loses his wage and has to pay a penalty $\frac{\overline{F}}{N}h^b(v)$. The bureaucrat has therefore to make a choice between two behaviors: to refuse the bribe and to make the logger pay the fine, or to accept it and to take the risk of being punished. The payoffs related to each strategy in each case are given in the following table.

	Not audited	Audited
Probability	$(1-\sigma)$	σ
Refuse the bribe	w	w
Accept the bribe	$w+B$	$B - \dfrac{\overline{F}}{N}h^b(v)$

The following figure shows the expected payoffs related to both strategies.

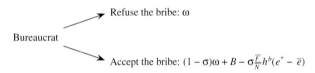

Bureaucrat
Refuse the bribe: ω
Accept the bribe: $(1-\sigma)\omega + B - \sigma\frac{\overline{F}}{N}h^b(e^* - \bar{e})$

We consider the situation in which accepting the bribe is the dominant strategy, implying:

$$B > \sigma\left(w + \frac{\overline{F}}{N}h^b(e^* - \bar{e})\right) \equiv \underline{B} \tag{3.4}$$

Indeed, the bureaucrat accepts the bribe if it is larger than the expected loss of being audited. $\underline{B}$ is therefore the reservation value of the bribe for the bureaucrat. The bureaucrat's net expected payoff is therefore his expected payoff of accepting the bribe, minus the payoff of refusing it:

$$\Psi^b = (1-\sigma)w + B - \sigma\frac{\overline{F}}{N}h^b(v) - w \tag{3.5}$$

If he accepts the bribe B, the bureaucrat is audited with probability σ and pays a fine $\frac{\overline{F}}{N}h^b(v)$. Moreover, he only keeps his wage w with probability

$1 - \sigma$ (i.e. if he is not audited). Finally, the *refuse* strategy generates a safe payoff of w.

3.3.2   Equilibrium harvest effort and bribe

The process to the equilibrium could be described as a *maximize-then-share-the-pie* process. First, the effort intensity of the logger is set in order to maximize the joint payoffs of both parties, taking $\overline{N}$, $\overline{F}$, and $\bar{e}$ as given. Second, the logger and the bureaucrat share the surplus through a Nash bargaining process.

Equilibrium harvest effort

Following Wilson and Damania (2005), the equilibrium harvest effort is set in order to maximize the joint net payoffs of the logger and the bureaucrat.

$$\max_{e} \; \Omega(e) = \psi^f + \psi^b = H\left(\frac{\overline{F}}{\overline{N}}; e\right) - H\left(\frac{\overline{F}}{\overline{N}}; \bar{e}\right) - \sigma w$$
$$+ B\left(1 - \frac{N^c}{\overline{N}}\right) - \sigma \frac{\overline{F}}{\overline{N}}\left[\frac{N^c}{\overline{N}} h^f(v) + h^b(v)\right] \tag{3.6}$$

The first-order condition gives:

$$\Omega_e = H_e - \sigma \frac{\overline{F}}{\overline{N}}\left[\frac{N^c}{\overline{N}} h_v^f + h_v^b\right] = 0 \tag{3.7}$$

The logger's optimal harvest effort $e^*(\overline{N}, \overline{F}, \bar{e}, N^c, \sigma, h_v^f, h_v^b)$ is implicitly given by equation (3.7). In equilibrium, it is set such that the marginal productivity of effort equals the marginal expected penalty.

Considering the factors influencing the logger's harvest effort, the parameters related to the control of the harvest volumes, σ, N^c, h_v^f, and h_v^b, unsurprisingly induce a smaller effort intensity in equilibrium: $e_x^* < 0$, for $x = \sigma, N^c, h_v^f, h_v^b$. Controlling the logger (and the bureaucrat) more intensively thus decreases the equilibrium effort intensity.

HARVEST QUOTA

The harvest quota $\bar{e}$ has a positive impact on the effective harvest effort. Indeed, a less stringent harvest quota reduces the extent of the potential fine:

$$e_{\bar{e}}^* = \frac{-\sigma \frac{\bar{F}}{N} \left(\frac{N^C}{N} h_v^f + h_v^b \right)}{H_{ee} - \sigma \frac{\bar{F}}{N} \left(\frac{N^C}{N} h_{vv}^f + h_{vv}^b \right)} > 0 \tag{3.8}$$

The stringency of the harvest quota is crucial to determining the extend of over-harvesting, and thus of the expected fine. A more stringent harvest quota naturally raises the amount that a logger would have to pay for a given harvest effort, and thus reduces the incentive to over-harvest.

HARVESTED FOREST

The impact of the size of the harvested forest $\bar{F}$ on the equilibrium harvest effort is given by:

$$e_{\bar{F}}^* = -\frac{\frac{H_{se}}{N} - \frac{\sigma}{N} \left[\frac{N^C}{N} h_v^f + h_v^b \right]}{H_{ee} - \sigma \frac{\bar{F}}{N} \left(\frac{N^C}{N} h_{vv}^f + h_{vv}^b \right)} \tag{3.9}$$

The influence of the size of concessions on the marginal productivity of effort is a key factor in determining the influence of the forest policy on the actual effort intensity. If larger concessions increase effort productivity, an increase in the size of the harvested forest increases the harvest effort of the loggers. In contrast, if effort effectiveness decreases with the size of concessions, it seems that there is a trade-off between primary forest preservation (through the size of the harvested forest) and over-harvesting (through harvest effort).

CONCENTRATION

The impact of $\bar{N}$ on the equilibrium effort level is

$$e_{\bar{N}}^* = -\frac{-\frac{\bar{F} H_{se}}{\bar{N}^2} + \sigma \frac{\bar{F}}{N} \left[\frac{1+\bar{N}}{\bar{N}^2} N^C h_v^f + h_v^b \right]}{H_{ee} - \sigma \frac{\bar{F}}{N} \left(\frac{N^C}{N} h_{vv}^f + h_{vv}^b \right)} \tag{3.10}$$

First, the fine is proportional to the concession size. Thus, smaller concessions (and a larger number of loggers) reduce the expected fine. Second, a large number of loggers reduces the probability of being inspected by the bureaucrat and audited by the authority, and thus reduces the expected marginal fine. This smaller expected fine is an incentive to raise the effort intensity and over-exploitation of the resource. Finally, the impact of $\bar{N}$ on the marginal productivity of effort is important. If an increase in the size of concessions tends to decrease the marginal productivity of effort ($H_{se} < 0$), a large number of loggers tends to increase the harvest effort ($H_{Ne} > 0$), and vice versa.

PROPOSITION 3.1 *A more stringent harvest quota tends to decrease the equilibrium harvest effort. Moreover, if the concession size has a negative impact on the marginal productivity of effort (or a positive but sufficiently small impact), the size of the harvested forest (a larger number of concessions) tends to decrease (increase) the equilibrium harvest effort. Conversely, if the effort marginal productivity reduces rapidly with the size of concessions, the size of the harvested forest (a larger number of concessions) increases (decreases) the equilibrium harvest effort.*

    Proof: See Appendix 3A.   □

Equilibrium bribe

The equilibrium bribe is set through a Nash bargaining process. Both parties are assumed to have the same bargaining power, so that they share equally the benefit of not respecting the harvest quota. We suppose here that the bargaining is successful. This implies that the equilibrium bribe must respect the reservation values described in equations (3.2) and (3.4).

    The equilibrium bribe is set by maximizing the Nash bargain:

$$\max_{B} \Psi^f \Psi^b = \left[H\left(\frac{\overline{F}}{\overline{N}}; e^* \right) - \frac{N^c}{\overline{N}} \left(B + \sigma \frac{\overline{F}}{\overline{N}} h^f(v) \right) - H\left(\frac{\overline{F}}{\overline{N}}; \bar{e} \right) \right]$$

$$\times \left[-\sigma w + B - \sigma \frac{\overline{F}}{\overline{N}} h^b(v) \right] \tag{3.11}$$

The first-order condition gives:

$$B = \frac{1}{2} \left[\frac{\overline{N}}{N^c} \left(H\left(\frac{\overline{F}}{\overline{N}}; e^* \right) - H\left(\frac{\overline{F}}{\overline{N}}; \bar{e} \right) \right) + \sigma w - \sigma \frac{\overline{F}}{\overline{N}} (h^f(v) - h^b(v)) \right] \tag{3.12}$$

This equilibrium bribe must lie in between the reservation values of both parties $[\underline{B}, \bar{B}]$, which implies that the benefit of not respecting the quota must exceed the global expected loss of being convicted:

$$H\left(\frac{\overline{F}}{\overline{N}}; e^* \right) - H\left(\frac{\overline{F}}{\overline{N}}; \bar{e} \right) > \frac{N^c}{\overline{N}} \sigma \left(w + \frac{\overline{F}}{\overline{N}} (h^f(v) - h^b(v)) \right) \tag{3.13}$$

First, in order to ensure that higher fines induce a decrease in the equilibrium bribe, we need to assume that $h^f > h^b$. Indeed, the punishment has to be more severe on the bribe giver. For otherwise, a higher fine on the recipient would incite the giver to raise the bribe to compensate for the recipient's expected fine. This assumption is consistent with the conclusions emerging from the literature (Mookherjee and Png 1995; Basu *et al.* 1992).

Second, the equilibrium bribe increases with the gain in revenue from not respecting the quota, $H(\frac{\overline{F}}{N}; e^*) - H(\frac{\overline{F}}{N}; \bar{e})$. Indeed, if the quota is stringent with respect to the net harvest function, the incentive to cheat is high, but corrupting is expensive, because of the extent of potential fines. Finally, the impact of the probability of being audited, σ, depends on what both agents have to lose: if the bureaucrat has more to lose than the logger ($w + \frac{\overline{F}}{N}h^b(v) > \frac{\overline{F}}{N}h^f(v)$), the bribe is increasing in σ and vice versa.

Third, the equilibrium bribe is positively correlated with the agent's wage. Indeed, it seems reasonable to assume that the bureaucrat is deprived of his wage if he is convicted of not enforcing the quota and being corrupt. Moreover, this assumption provides the insight that a well-paid bureaucrat is more expensive to corrupt, simply because he has more to lose.

Finally, the bribe reduces with the number of loggers inspected by the bureaucrat N^c. Indeed, N^c raises the probability of being inspected, and thus reduces the expected benefit obtained by the logger from his extra effort, which naturally reduces its incentive to cheat.

Finally, the impact of the number of concessions is not clear:

$$B_{\overline{N}} = \frac{1}{2}\left[\frac{1}{N^c}\left(H\left(\frac{\overline{F}}{N}; e^*\right) - H\left(\frac{\overline{F}}{N}; \bar{e}\right)\right) + \frac{\overline{F}}{N^c}\left(H_s\left(\frac{\overline{F}}{N}, \bar{e}\right)\right.\right.$$
$$\left.\left. - H_s\left(\frac{\overline{F}}{N}, e^*\right)\right) + \sigma\frac{\overline{F}}{N^2}(h^f(v) - h^b(v))\right] \qquad (3.14)$$

The first part of the equation, $H(\frac{\overline{F}}{N}; e^*) - H(\frac{\overline{F}}{N}; \bar{e})$, which corresponds to the productive incentive to cheat, is positive. The second part, $H_s(\frac{\overline{F}}{N}, \bar{e}) - H_s(\frac{\overline{F}}{N}, e^*)$, depends on the cross derivative of the net harvest function H_{se}. As $\bar{e} < e^*$, this second part of the equation is also positive, if $H_{se} < 0$. Finally, the third part of the equation expresses the impact of the concession size on the fine, which is positive. Overall, a larger number of concessions increases the equilibrium bribe if the impact of the size of concessions on the net marginal productivity of effort is negative (or positive but sufficiently small).

3.4   Lobbying and the forest policy design

Proceeding backward, we now analyze the forest policy ($\overline{N}$, $\overline{F}$ and $\bar{e}$) choice process (the socially optimal policy is given in Appendix 3B).

An exogenous number of loggers N_l acts as one lobby, the aim of which is to get a less stringent forest policy. The lobby's objective thus consists of increasing the size of the forest to exploit $\overline{F}$ and the harvest quota $\bar{e}$, and setting a number of concessions $\overline{N}$ close to the number of loggers in the lobby. N_l may represent the number of political allies that the policy-maker may reward.

Neither the policy-maker nor the lobby consider the impact of the forest policy instruments on bureaucratic corruption. In that sense, they have a naive point of view concerning the forest policy and implicitly assume that the policy is enforced. This assumption makes sense if we consider the fact that public policies are usually chosen on the implicit assumption that they will be enforced. The fact that bureaucratic corruption may influence the policy choice of the government is treated in Amacher *et al.* (2008).

The total forest area is set to 1. Thus, $\overline{F}$ is the share of the forest to be harvested, while $1 - \overline{F}$ represents protected primary forest.

3.4.1   The logger–policy-maker interaction

To address this issue, we build on Grossman and Helpman (1994). The policy-maker's objective function is a weighted sum of social welfare and bribes:

$$G(F, N, e) = \alpha W \left(N H \left(\frac{F}{N}; e \right); (1 - F); e \right) + (1 - \alpha)C(F, N, e)$$

(3.15)

W is the social welfare function. It is increasing in the total harvested volumes. Moreover, the social welfare function is increasing in the size of primary protected forests, $1 - F$ (and thus decreasing in the size of harvested forest), because of the environmental services provided, such as biodiversity conservation or hydrological benefits. Finally, the social welfare function is decreasing in the harvest effort, assimilated to environmental degradation (biodiversity loss, erosion, wildlife habitat degradation): $W_H > 0$, $W_{(1-F)} > 0$, $W_e < 0$, $W_{HH} < 0$, $W_{(1-F)(1-F)} < 0$, and $W_{ee} < 0$.

$1 - \alpha$ is the degree of corruptibility of the policy-maker and $C(F, N, e)$ is the bribe schedule offered by the lobby to the policy-maker. The bribe is increasing in the size of the harvested forest and the harvest quota: $C_F > 0$, $C_e > 0$.

Moreover, the bribe is increasing in the number of concessions, as long as it is smaller than the number of lobbying loggers: $C_N > 0$, for $N < N_l$; $C_N = 0$, for $N \geq N_l$. The shape and sign of the bribe schedule $C(N)$ depend on the relationship between the policy-maker and the lobbying loggers. As an extreme case, if the political allies of the policy-maker are very powerful and can put enough pressure on the policy-maker, the choice of the number of concessions is not a choice anymore, but becomes a constraint for the policy-maker. In this case: $C(N) < 0$, for $\overline{N} < N_l$; and $C(N) = 0$, for $\overline{N} \geq N_l$.

The forestry sector acts as a lobby. We define the lobby's degree of satisfaction as the share of lobbying loggers receiving a concession: $\frac{N}{N_l}$. The lobby's payoff increases with its degree of satisfaction and the total net harvest volumes, and decreases with the bribe paid to the policy-maker. The lobby's payoff therefore captures a dilution affect: it is more difficult to satisfy the whole lobby if it is composed of a large number of loggers:

$$\Pi(F, N, e) = \frac{N^2}{N_l} H\left(\frac{F}{N}; e\right) - (1 + \lambda(N_l))C(F, N, e) \tag{3.16}$$

The effect of the number of loggers N_l on the lobby coordination is captured by $\lambda(N_l)$, which corresponds to the coordination costs of the lobby and the costs due to free-rider behaviors by the lobby members. This setup follows Laffont and Tirole (1991) and Fredriksson *et al.* (2004). It is assumed that $\lambda_{N_l} > 0$.

3.4.2 Equilibrium forest policy

The equilibrium consists of the size of the harvested forest $\overline{F}$, the harvest quota $\bar{e}$, and the number of concessions $\overline{N}$. Overall, it is easy to see that a more corrupt policy-maker (with low α) puts more weight on the lobby's objective and thus designs a less stringent forest policy. The conditions for equilibrium are consistent with the political economy literature.

Equilibrium harvest quota

First, the equilibrium harvest quota $\bar{e}$ maximizes both (i) $G(e)$ and (ii) $G(e) + \Pi(e)$, and the first-order conditions satisfy:

(i) $\alpha W_H H_e + \alpha W_e + (1 - \alpha)C_e = 0$;
(ii) $\alpha W_H H_e + \alpha W_e + (1 - \alpha)C_e + \frac{\overline{N}^2}{N_l} H_e - (1 + \lambda(N_l))C_e = 0$.

$\bar{e}$ is implicitly given by:

$$\left((1-\alpha)\frac{\overline{N}^2}{N_l} + \alpha(1+\lambda(N_l))W_H\right)H_e = -\alpha(1+\lambda(N_l))W_e \qquad (3.17)$$

IMPACT OF THE NUMBER OF LOBBYING LOGGERS N_L ON THE EQUILIBRIUM HARVEST QUOTA $\bar{E}$

The impact of the number of lobbying loggers is given by:

$$\bar{e}_{N_l} = \frac{-((1-\alpha)\frac{\overline{N}^2}{N_l})^2 H_e + \lambda_{N_l}\alpha(W_H H_e + W_e)}{(1-\alpha)\frac{\overline{N}^2}{N_l}H_{ee} + \alpha(1+\lambda(N_l))(W_H H_{ee} + W_{ee})} > 0 \qquad (3.18)$$

Equilibrium size of harvested forest

$\overline{F}$ maximizes both (i) $G(F)$ and (ii) $G(F) + \Pi(F)$. The first-order conditions are:

(i) $\alpha W_H H_s - \alpha W_{(1-F)} + (1-\alpha)C_F = 0$ \qquad (3.19)

(ii) $\alpha W_H H_s - \alpha W_{(1-F)} + (1-\alpha)C_F + \dfrac{NH_s}{N_l} - (1+\lambda(N_l))C_F = 0$

$$\qquad (3.20)$$

These imply that

$$\left((1-\alpha)\frac{\overline{N}}{N_l(1+\lambda(N_l))} + \alpha W_H\right)H_s = \alpha W_{(1-F)} \qquad (3.21)$$

which gives implicitly the equilibrium size of the harvested forest $\overline{F}$. A more corrupt policy-maker therefore tends unsurprisingly to put less weight on social welfare and more weight on the lobby's harvest. Thus, the equilibrium size of the harvested forest is greater than the social optimum.

IMPACT OF THE NUMBER OF LOBBYING LOGGERS N_L ON THE EQUILIBRIUM SIZE OF HARVESTED FOREST

The impact of N_l on $\overline{F}$ is given by

$$\overline{F}_{N_l} = \frac{-\frac{(1+\lambda(N_l))+N_l\lambda_{N_l}}{(N_l(1+\lambda(N_l)))^2}\overline{N}H_s}{(1-\alpha)\frac{H_{ss}}{N_l(1+\lambda(N_l))} + \alpha\left(\frac{W_H H_{ss}}{N} + W_{(1-F)(1-F)}\right)} > 0 \qquad (3.22)$$

Equilibrium number of concessions

The choice of the number of concessions allocated $\overline{N}$ follows the same analysis. $\overline{N}$ maximizes both (i) $G(N)$ and (ii) $G(N) + \Pi(N)$, and the first-order conditions satisfy:

(i) $\alpha W_H(H(\frac{F}{N}; e) - \frac{F}{N^2} H_s) + (1 - \alpha)C_N = 0$;

(ii) $\alpha W_H(H(\frac{F}{N}; e) - \frac{F}{N^2} H_s) + (1 - \alpha)C_N + \frac{1}{N_l}(2NH(\frac{F}{N}; e) - FH_s) - (1 + \lambda(N_l))C_N = 0$.

The equilibrium number of concessions $\overline{N}$ is implicitly given by:

$$
\left((1 - \alpha)\frac{2\overline{N}}{N_l(1 + \lambda(N_l))} + \alpha W_H \right) H\left(\frac{\overline{F}}{\overline{N}}; e \right)
$$
$$
= \left((1 - \alpha)\frac{1}{N_l(1 + \lambda(N_l))} + \alpha W_H \right) \overline{F} H_s \qquad (3.23)
$$

IMPACT OF THE NUMBER OF LOBBYING LOGGERS N_L ON THE EQUILIBRIUM NUMBER OF CONCESSIONS $\overline{N}$

The impact of the number of lobbying loggers is given by

$$
\overline{N}_{N_l} = \frac{\frac{(1+\lambda(N_l))+N_l\lambda_{N_l}}{(N_l(1+\lambda(N_l)))^2} 2\overline{N}\left(H\left(\frac{F}{N}; e\right) - \overline{F}H_s\right)}{\frac{2(1-\alpha)}{N_l(1+\lambda(N_l))} H\left(\frac{F}{N}; e\right) - \left(\frac{2(1-\alpha)\overline{N}}{N_l(1+\lambda(N_l))} + \alpha W_H\right)\frac{\overline{F}}{N^2} H_s + \left(\frac{(1-\alpha)}{N_l(1+\lambda(N_l))} + \alpha W_H\right)\left(\frac{\overline{F}}{N}\right)^2 H_{ss}^{-1}} > 0
$$
$$
(3.24)
$$

PROPOSITION 3.2 *A more corrupt policy-maker sets a more permissive forest policy. Moreover, a larger number of lobbying loggers tends to increase the equilibrium harvest quota, the size of the harvested forest, the equilibrium number of concess ions.*

Proof: See Appendix 3C. □

Therefore, we can assume in this context that a larger number of political allies to reward tends to increase policy-maker corruption for the whole forest policy.

3.5 How size of concessions may influence systemic corruption

The literature on corruption often supposes that corruption is systemic: a corrupt policy-maker often coexists with a corrupt bureaucracy. The model presented here allows us to consider the relationship between both types of corruption in the context of forest harvesting.

A crucial element is how marginal productivity of effort evolves with the size of concessions.

The case of marginal effort productivity *decreasing* with the size of concessions is consistent for countries with less accessible forest resources and small infrastructure implementation (e.g. Chile, Congo Basin). Policy-maker corruption tends to increase the size of the harvested forest, the number of concessions and the harvest quota. Considering Proposition 3.1, a larger harvested forest tends to decrease the equilibrium harvest intensity, and a less stringent harvest quota and a larger number of concessions increase harvest intensity. Therefore, policy-maker corruption tends to enhance the impact of bureaucratic corruption for two key forest policy instruments and to decrease it for the third.

The net effect depends on two types of elasticities: the elasticity of equilibrium harvest (e^*) to the policy instruments ($\bar{e}$, $\overline{N}$, $\overline{F}$), and the elasticity of the policy instruments to corruption (α). It is not possible to determine the net impact under the model described here, because deriving elasticities requires a less general specification of the harvesting and social welfare functions.

Policy-maker corruption (PMC) enhances bureaucratic corruption (BC) through harvest intensity and the number of concessions, while decreasing it through the size of the harvested forest. Overall, policy-maker corruption thus increases the impact of bureaucratic corruption if

$$\underbrace{\overbrace{\left[\frac{\partial \bar{e}}{\partial \alpha}\frac{\alpha}{\bar{e}}\right]}^{-}\overbrace{\left[\frac{\partial e^*}{\partial \bar{e}}\frac{\bar{e}}{e^*}\right]}^{+} + \overbrace{\left[\frac{\partial \overline{N}}{\partial \alpha}\frac{\alpha}{\overline{N}}\right]}^{-}\overbrace{\left[\frac{\partial e^*}{\partial \overline{N}}\frac{\overline{N}}{e^*}\right]}^{+}}_{PMC \nearrow BC} + \underbrace{\overbrace{\left[\frac{\partial \overline{F}}{\partial \alpha}\frac{\alpha}{\overline{F}}\right]}^{-}\overbrace{\left[\frac{\partial e^*}{\partial \overline{F}}\frac{\overline{F}}{e^*}\right]}^{-}}_{PMC \searrow BC} < 0$$

(3.25)

The case of marginal effort productivity *increasing* with the size of concessions corresponds to countries with more accessible forest resources and well-implemented infrastructure (e.g. Brazil, Indonesia). In this case, from Proposition 3.2, a larger harvested forest and less stringent harvest quota tend to increase the equilibrium harvest intensity and a larger number of concessions tends to decrease harvest intensity. Therefore, government corruption also enhances the impact of bureaucratic corruption for two key forest policy instruments and to decrease it for the third. Overall, policy-maker corruption thus increases the impact of bureaucratic corruption if

$$\underbrace{\left[\overset{-}{\frac{\partial \bar{e}}{\partial \alpha}\frac{\alpha}{\bar{e}}}\right]\left[\overset{+}{\frac{\partial e^*}{\partial \bar{e}}\frac{\bar{e}}{e^*}}\right]}_{PMC \nearrow BC} + \underbrace{\left[\overset{-}{\frac{\partial \bar{F}}{\partial \alpha}\frac{\alpha}{\bar{F}}}\right]\left[\overset{+}{\frac{\partial e^*}{\partial \bar{F}}\frac{\bar{F}}{e^*}}\right]}_{} + \underbrace{\left[\overset{-}{\frac{\partial \bar{N}}{\partial \alpha}\frac{\alpha}{\bar{N}}}\right]\left[\overset{-}{\frac{\partial e^*}{\partial \bar{N}}\frac{\bar{N}}{e^*}}\right]}_{PMC \searrow BC} < 0$$

$$(3.26)$$

3.6 Conclusion

This chapter explores the links between size of concessions, systemic corruption and forest harvesting. Corruption may occur at different scales of governments. First, logging firms may bribe the bureaucrat in charge of the inspection, so that he underreports the harvest volume. Second, a lobby composed of several loggers may bribe the policy-maker to set a more permissive forest policy.

In the first case of bureaucratic corruption, the size of concessions constitute a key variable. If the harvest marginal productivity decreases with the size of concessions (or increases slightly), a forestry sector composed of a large number of small concessions tends to increase the impact of corruption on forest over-exploitation. Indeed, a large number of logging firms reduces the control capacity of the civil agency. Moreover, in this case, small concessions (i.e. a large number of loggers) appear to be an incentive for harvest intensification. On the other hand, more stringent harvest quota decrease the incentive to over-harvest. Finally, a larger harvested forest tends to decrease the harvest intensity, which supports the idea of a trade-off between primary forest conservation and over-harvesting: a larger harvested forest is related to a smaller protected area, but tends to decrease over-harvesting. In contrast, if the marginal productivity of effort increases with the size of concessions, then small concessions and a larger harvested forest tend to decrease over-harvesting and the impact of bureaucratic corruption.

In the second case of policy-maker corruption, a corrupt policy-maker tends to set a larger harvested forest, a less stringent harvest quota and a larger number of concessions. Moreover, a larger number of lobbying loggers (or political allies) is related to less stringent forest policies.

Those two sets of results allow us to consider corruption as a systemic problem. Indeed, a corrupt policy-maker tends to set a less stringent forest policy. Less stringent harvest quotas are always related to more intensive equilibrium harvest effort. If the marginal productivity of effort decreases with the size of concessions, a larger number of concessions is also positively related to over-harvesting. If the marginal productivity of effort increases with the size of concessions, policy-maker corruption enhances the impact of bureaucratic corruption through the size of the harvested forest. Overall, this chapter partly supports the idea of systemic corruption, through two key forest policy instruments. The net impact of policy-maker corruption on bureaucratic corruption depends on the specification of net harvest function.

Two main policy implications are underlined in this chapter. First, scale effects need to be taken into account when considering bureaucratic corruption. If the marginal productivity of effort increases with the size of concessions, then a larger number of small concessions may help to restrain the impact of "petty" corruption. Second, policy-maker and bureaucratic corruption need to be considered as a whole. More precisely, the design of the forest policy may have an impact on the extent of bureaucratic corruption.

This model suffers from a number of limitations, offering scope for further research. A crucial limitation is that loggers and concessions are assumed to be homogeneous in size. However, in real life, small and large concessions often coexist. Thus, it could be interesting to consider the difference in corruption patterns between heterogeneous loggers. For example, small loggers might choose to bribe bureaucrats, while large loggers find ut more profitable to bribe policy-makers directly.

Moreover, the process of allocation of concessions is not modeled explicitly in this chapter. Nevertheless, it is an important pattern of corruption and forest exploitation in developing countries. Indeed, corrupt regimes often use these allocation processes to reward their political allies or to increase the wealth of their friends or family. In this context, concessions would be given according to the number of these allies and their "worthiness", which would determine the size of concessions. Moreover, logging firms may compete for allocations.

Appendix 3A: Proof of Proposition 3.1

HARVEST QUOTA

In equation (3.8), both the numerator and the denominator are unambiguously negative. Thus, a more stringent harvest quota reduces the equilibrium harvest effort: $e_{\bar{e}}^* > 0$.

HARVESTED FOREST

In equation (3.9), the denominator is unambiguously negative. Thus, the sign of the equation is of the sign of the numerator. The equilibrium harvest effort is therefore decreasing with the size of the harvested forest, $e_{\bar{F}}^* > 0$, if

$$H_{se} < \sigma \left[\frac{N^c}{\overline{N}} h_v^f + h_v^b \right] \qquad (3.27)$$

NUMBER OF CONCESSIONS

The sign of the denominator being unambiguously negative, equation (3.10) has the sign of $\frac{-\overline{F} H_{se}}{\overline{N}^2} + \sigma \frac{\overline{F}}{\overline{N}} [\frac{1+\overline{N}}{\overline{N}^2} N^c h_v^f + h_v^b]$. Thus, the condition for the equilibrium harvest effort to increase with the number of harvesting firms, $e_{\overline{N}}^* > 0$, is

$$H_{se} < \sigma \overline{N} \left[\frac{1 + \overline{N}}{\overline{N}^2} N^c h_v^f + h_v^b \right] \qquad (3.28)$$

Appendix 3B: Socially optimal policy

The socially optimal forest policy is given for a non-corrupt policy-maker: $\alpha = 1$. The socially optimal size of the harvested forest is implicitly given by:

$$W_H H_s = W_{(1-F)} \qquad (3.29)$$

The socially optimal number of concessions is implicitly given by:

$$H \left(\frac{\overline{F}}{\overline{N}}; e \right) = \overline{F} H_s \qquad (3.30)$$

The socially optimal harvest quota is implicitly given by:

$$W_H H_e + W_e = 0 \qquad (3.31)$$

Appendix 3C: Proof of Proposition 3.2

$\bar{e}_{N_l} > 0$. Note from equation (3.23) that $(1 - \alpha) \frac{\overline{N}^2}{N_l} + \alpha(1 + \lambda(N_l)) > \alpha(1 + \lambda(N_l))$, which implies that: $W_H H_e < -W_e$. Thus, the numerator is negative. Moreover, by assumption, $H_{ee} < 0$, $W_H > 0$ and $W_{ee} < 0$. Thus, the denominator is also negative. Overall, a larger number of lobbying loggers thus increases the equilibrium harvest quota.

$\overline{F}_{N_l} > 0$. We know that, by assumption, $\lambda(N_l) > 0$, $\lambda_{N_l} > 0$, and $H_s > 0$. Thus, the numerator of equation (3.20) is negative. Moreover, by assumption, $H_{ss} < 0$, $W_H > 0$, and $W_{(1-F)(1-F)}$. Therefore, the denominator is also negative. Thus, $\overline{F}_{N_l} > 0$.

$\overline{N}_{N_l} > 0$. Note from equation (3.21), that: $(\frac{2(1-\alpha)\overline{N}}{N_l(1+\lambda(N_l))} + \alpha W_H) >$
$(\frac{(1-\alpha)}{N_l(1+\lambda(N_l))} + \alpha W_H)$. Which implies necessarily that, in equilibrium:
$H(\frac{F}{N}; e) < \overline{F}H_s$. This result implies that both the numerator and denominator of equation (3.22) are negative, which proves that $\overline{N}_{N_l} > 0$.

References

Amacher, G. S. (2006) Corruption: A challenge for economists interested in forest policy design. *Journal of Forest Economics*, 12(2): 85–9.

Amacher, G., Ollikainen, M. and Koskela, E. (2008) Corruption and forests concessions. Working Paper, Virginia Polytechnic Institute and State University.

Barbier, E., Damania, R. and Leonard, D. (2005) Corruption, trade and resource conversion. *Journal of Environmental Economics and Management*, 50(2): 229–46.

Basu, K., Bhattacharya, S. and Mishra, A. (1992) Notes on bribery and the control of corruption. *Journal of Public Economics*, 48: 349–59.

Callister, D. (1999) Corrupt and illegal activities in the forestry sector: Current understandings, and implications for world bank forest policy. World Bank.

Contreras-Hermosilla, A. (2001) Law compliance in the forestry sector. World Bank. Washington, DC.

Dudley, N., Jeanrenaud, J. and Sullivan, F. (1995) Bad harvest? The timber trade and the degradation of the world's forests. WWF-UK, London.

Eerola, E. (2004) Forest conservation – too much or too little? A political economy model. *Environmental and Resource Economics*, 27: 391–407.

Fredriksson, P., Vollebergh, H. and Djikgraaf, E. (2004) Corruption and energy efficiency in OECD countries: theory and evidence. *Journal of Environmental Economics and Management*, 47: 207–31.

Gray, J. (2000) Forest concessions: Experience and lessons from countries around the world.

IUFRO International Symposium on Integrated Management of Neotropical Rain Forests by Industries and Communities. Belém, Brazil.

Gray, J. (2002) Forest concessions policies and sustainable forest management of tropical forests. *World Bank*. Washington, DC.

Grossman, G. and Helpman, E. (1994) Protection for sale. *American Economic Review*, 84(4): 833–50.

Harris White, B. (1996) Liberalization and corruption. *IDS Bulletin*, 2/1996.

Karsenty, A. (2007) Overview of industrial forest concessions and concession-based industry in Central and West Africa and consideration of alternatives. Rights and Resources Initiative (Washington), http://www.rightsandresources.org/

Laffont, J. and Tirole, J. (1991) The politics of government decision-making: a theory of regulatory capture. *Quaterly Journal of Economics*, 106: 1089–1127.

Mookherjee, D. and Png, I. (1995) Corruptible law enforcers: how should they be compensated? *Economic Journal*, 105: 145–59.

Rose-Ackerman, S. (1978) *Corruption: A Study in Political Economy*. New York: Academic Press.

Rose-Ackerman, S. (1999) *Corruption and Government: Causes, Consequences and Reform*. New York. Cambridge University Press.

Ruiz Perez, M., de Blas, D., Nasi, R., Sayer, J., Sassen, M., Angoue, C., Gami, N., Ndoye, O., Ngono, G., Nguinguiri, J., Nzala, D. and Toirambe, B. and Yalibanda, Y. (2005) Logging in the Congo Basin: a multi-country characterization of timber companies. *Forest Ecology and Management*, 214: 221–36.

Transparency International (2003) *Global Corruption Report 2003*. www.globalcorruptionreport.org.

Wilson, J. and Damania, R. (2005) Corruption, political competition and environmental policy. *Journal of Environmental Economics and Management*, 49: 516–35.

Winbourne, S. (2002) Corruption and the environment. Management System International/United States Agency for International Development.

World Bank (2000) Anticorruption in transition: A contribution to the policy debate. World Bank, Washington, DC.

4 Unsustainable timber harvesting, deforestation and the role of certification

This chapter was written with Olivier Damette (Université Paris 12) and published in *Ecological Economics* 70(6) (2011).

4.1 Introduction

Every year, about 13 million hectares of forest are converted to other land uses (FAO 2010), leading to biodiversity losses, soil erosion, and massive CO_2 emissions. The investigation of the processes of deforestation has provided a broad literature, both at macro and micro levels. Angelsen and Kaimowitz (1999) give an extensive overview of the direct and underlying causes of deforestation, among which are agricultural prices and technologies, timber prices, institutions, and property rights. Globally, most studies agree upon the fact that agricultural expansion is the leading direct factor of deforestation: farmers and firms convert forests to agriculture. It has been estimated that up to 70 percent of deforestation was related to agricultural expansion at the forest frontiers (UNEP 2003). Recent work focusing on country-level studies has shown that higher corruption and lower institutional quality (Nguyen Van and Azomahou 2007), higher real exchange rates (Arcand *et al.* 2008), and development (Culas 2007; Ewers 2006; Rudel *et al.* 2005) can indirectly increase deforestation. Combes Motel *et al.* (2009) distinguish structural and policy-related deforestation factors. Nevertheless, Scrieciu (2007) notes the fact that autocorrelation is a major problem usually not considered in studies dealing with global analysis of the deforestation factors. The author shows that taking autocorrelation into account significantly decreases the strength of the empirical results.

At the same time, demand for timber products is rapidly increasing, essentially in the developing world. FAO projections mention an annual worldwide consumption increase of 1.5 percent for sawnwood, 3.3 percent for wood-based panels, and 3 percent for paper for the 2005–20 period (FAO 2009). A natural question is then whether forest harvesting is sustainable worldwide. Sustainable forest harvesting should not be related to deforestation, which is defined as a radical removal of vegetation, to less than 10 percent crown cover. This definition refers to a change in the land use and long-term removal of tree cover (Angelsen and Kaimowitz 1999). If it is sustainable, harvested timber should either come from secondary forest plantations, or selected harvest in natural forests concessions. In both cases, the harvested area should be replanted or left to recover. In any case, it should not be related to a change in the land use.

It follows that if timber harvesting is related to deforestation, this gives the intuition that demand for timber products is partially fulfilled with timber harvested in the deforestation process, and not in relation to sustainable forest harvesting. In this sense, harvested timber may be considered as a by-product of deforestation.

This chapter assesses the following issues. Is forest harvesting related to deforestation? Are timber products a by-product of deforestation? Do countries with more important forest sectors experience more deforestation than others? Does timber certification play a key role in favoring sustainable harvesting? To treat those questions, we use panel-data and cross-country analysis, investigating the links between forestry sectors, certification, and deforestation.

Section 4.2 develops the potential links between deforestation and timber harvesting. Section 4.3 presents a panel-data analysis of the links between timber harvesting and deforestation. In Section 4.4, the capability of timber certification to increase timber harvesting sustainability is considered, and Section 4.5 concludes.

4.2 Is timber harvesting sustainable?

Agricultural expansion is the major cause of deforestation. It follows that timber over-harvesting is usually not considered as a leading factor of deforestation. Nevertheless, investigating the links between timber harvesting and deforestation is an interesting issue, related to timber harvesting sustainability.

Sustainable forest management is defined as "the stewardship and use of forests and forest lands in a way, and at a rate, that maintains their biological diversity, productivity, regeneration capacity, vitality and their potential to fulfil, now and in the future, relevant ecological economic and social functions, at local, national and global levels, and that does not cause damage on other ecosystems" (Helsinki Resolution H1, in Mayer 2000). Obviously, from this definition, the decrease in forest area cannot be related to sustainable forest management, since deforestation is related to a decrease in biodiversity and productivity.

Demand for timber products could be fulfilled by two channels. On the one hand, timber products can be provided by harvesting timber in a sustainable manner. In this case, timber may come from concessions in secondary forests plantations, or from selected harvest in natural forests. In the first case of dedicated forest plantations, the harvested area may be replanted or left regrown. In the case of selected natural timber harvesting, the harvested area is usually left regrown. In both cases, sustainable harvest does not imply long-term change in the land use.

On the other hand, timber products may come from unsustainable practices. The word "unsustainable" may have two meanings here. First, trees that are cut down during the agricultural expansion process can be considered as by-products of deforestation. This is the case when deforestation is taking place at agricultural frontiers. Timber harvesting is here unsustainable in the sense that it cannot be sustained in the long run. Second, forests may be cut down for their timber, not replaced, and then switched to other uses. Deforestation results here from timber production practices that are unsustainable by themselves. Note here that unsustainable timber harvesting is a factor of deforestation only in the second case, and not in the first one. However, it is difficult to distinguish both cases, since deforestation at agricultural frontiers and logging frequently coexist in less developed countries. Nevertheless, in both cases, unsustainable timber harvesting is positively related to deforestation. Finding this type of relationship would then give the intuition that timber harvesting is not sustainable, considering both meanings that we express here.

This issue is particularly relevant when considering the projected evolution of demand for timber products in the developing world. For the 2005–20 period, demographic and economic growth should lead to important increases in timber consumption in many regions of the developing world (FAO 2009). Sawnwood consumption should increase by 2.8 percent per year in Africa and 2.5 percent in Western and Central Asia. Wood-based panels consumption should have a yearly increase of 4.8 percent in Asia and the Pacific and 4.5 percent in Western and Central Asia. Demand for paper may increase up to 4.6 percent per year in Africa, 4.1 percent per year in Asia and the Pacific, and 4 percent per year in Western and Central Asia. Finally, industrial roundwood consumption should increase by 3.1 percent per year in Asia and the Pacific. It is then an important and interesting issue to investigate by which of the two channels demand for timber products is fulfilled.

4.3   A panel-data analysis of the links between timber harvesting and deforestation

We first present our econometric model. Then we discuss econometric issues. Finally, we analyze the results.

4.3.1 Presentation of the panel-data analysis

Econometric model

The literature on deforestation drivers shows that there is no single theoretical model to explain the complexity of the deforestation process. In addition, the macroeconomic explanations are not applicable uniformly over time and across space but are location- and context-specific. Therefore, we are confronted with an omitted variables problem. The main interest of using panel-data models is in obtaining consistent estimators in the presence of omitted variables and considering the heterogeneity of the individuals. To this end, we proceed by including an unobserved time constant variable capturing unobserved features of each country and individual motivations to deforest. These individual motivations are considered as given and do not change over time.

We regress our deforestation proxy (*Deforestation*) on our indicator of timber harvesting (*Harvest$_{it}$*) and other potential explanatory variables (*X*):

$$Deforestation_{it} = \alpha_i + \beta_1 Harvest_{it} + \beta_2 X_{it} + u_{it} \qquad (4.1)$$

Subscript *i* refers to the country and *t* is the year considered. α_i captures the unobserved component.

Data and expected results

Our sample consists of a strong balanced panel of 87 countries (both developing and developed countries) covering the 1972–94 period (2,001 observations). A full data description is given in Appendix 4A.

Our deforestation indicator is the yearly decrease in forest cover (source: FAO) over the sample period. The average deforestation rate is positive (0.187 percent), which means that forests are being lost at a global scale. We note that extreme yearly deforestation rates may reflect outliers (from -28 percent to 22.8 percent). Indeed, as many studies have done before us, we acknowledge the fact that deforestation data at a country level and over a 22-year period may be weak. Moreover, definitions of forests and measurement of forest cover have changed over the period. We chose nevertheless to use this database to be able to compare our results with those of similar studies (Arcand *et al.* 2008; Nguyen Van and Azomahou 2007). Note in addition that we also use recent data (2005–10) in the cross-country part of the chapter and derive very similar results. Finally, we used a variable of arable cropland expansion (source: WRI) as a proxy for deforestation to check the robustness of our panel results.

The variable *Harvest* may take two forms. First, *Harvest-volume* is the log of the volume of roundwood harvested (source: FAO). Conversely, *Harvest-value* is the log of the volume of roundwood harvested times a timber price index (i.e. the yearly average price in the country, source: FAO). Then *Harvest-volume* only presents the links between harvesting and deforestation, while *Harvest-value* also has a price element that may be related to deforestation. Indeed, higher timber prices may either (i) give an incentive to increase harvest and potentially deforestation, or (ii) give an incentive to invest in sustainable forest management and then to protect forests. Both variables are normalized to GDP (source: World Bank tables). Then, *Harvest-value* may also be interpreted as a proxy for the forestry sector's importance in the country's economy. As discussed before, sustainable timber harvesting should not be related to the forest cover and deforestation (no expected significant sign), while unsustainable timber harvesting is positively linked to deforestation (expected sign +). Indeed, the FAO definition of the forest cover is: "Land spanning more than 0.5 hectares with trees higher than 5 meters and a canopy cover of more than 10 percent." Harvest is related to deforestation only if the cover decreases to less than 10 percent.

Our set of control variables is consistent with the literature on the deforestation factors. First, institutional quality is frequently mentioned as a key element explaining deforestation: countries with poorer institutions (higher corruption, lower bureaucratic effectiveness) usually experience higher deforestation rates. Indeed, corruption and rent-seeking activities are frequently cited factors of timber over-harvesting in developing countries (Amacher 2006; Chapter 3, this volume). More generally, poor institutional quality is likely to induce poor policy-making, which generates unsustainable forest management. Overall, many empirical analysis find that better institutions reduce deforestation (Arcand *et al.* 2008; Culas 2007; Nguyen Van and Azomahou 2007). We approximate institutional quality, using two indicators from the Freedom House: political rights and civil liberties. As in Bhattarai and Hamming (2001) and Nguyen Van and Azomahou (2007), we add the values of the two indicators, and compute an overall index of political institutions. This method avoids potential collinearity issues between civil liberties and political rights variables. A low score of this variable (the minimum value is 2; the maximum value is 14) is related to better institutional credibility and higher freedom (*Institutions*; expected sign +). As noticed by Arcand *et al.* (2008), "[g]iven that, in the context of deforestation, it is an indicator of institutions associated with property rights that one needs, the Freedom House index is a less appropriate proxy." We nevertheless chose this proxy, since it is available over our period of interest, in contrast to other institutional indicators.[1]

Second, we consider a potential Kuznets curve for deforestation (*GDP*, expected sign +; *GDP*², expected sign −), which is already covered in the literature (Arcand *et al.* 2008; Culas 2007; Nguyen Van and Azomahou 2007, among others). Third, we consider the annual growth rate of GDP (source: Penn World Table 6.1) as a potential explanatory variable, to consider the potential global influence of economic activity on the deforestation process (*Growth*; no expected sign). Fourth, we consider the fact that population density (source: World Bank tables) may be positively related to deforestation (Nguyen Van and Azomahou 2007; Combes Motel *et al.* 2009): higher population density is likely to be related to more intensive land and food needs, which could lead to more land conversion (*Density*, expected sign +).

Finally, the forest transition hypothesis is likely to influence deforestation (Rudel *et al.* 2005; Ewers 2006). Deforestation is perceived cheaper for a country with large forest endowments. The implicit idea is that the net benefit (or cost) of deforesting is decreasing (increasing) in forest scarcity. Net benefit of deforestation includes the benefit of agricultural expansion and the environmental costs of reducing the forest cover. Thus, we expect a positive impact of forest endowments on deforestation (*ForestCover*, expected sign +).[2]

The distributions of harvest volume, GDP, population density and growth are highly dispersed because the database contains both developing and developed countries. Then we report in Appendix 4A the descriptive statistics concerning developed and developing countries, respectively. The results reveal a significant heterogeneity of the macroeconomic variables across low- and high-income countries. Furthermore, we conducted different regressions across the level of development of the countries.

Econometric methodology

In our strongly balanced short panel, N is sufficiently large relative to T ($N = 87$, $T = 22$). That kind of panel largely determines the econometric methodology used thereafter. When we make the assumption of fixed T and N grows without bounds, we can consequently assume rough independence in the cross-section. Our asymptotic analysis should provide suitable approximations, as stressed by Wooldridge (2002a, b).

Before carrying out the estimates of our empirical model, it is useful to discuss briefly the nature of the unobserved component. The term α_i can be viewed as a random or fixed effect. In our study, it is reasonable to assume that some explanatory variables (GDP, population density) are correlated with the unobserved features of each country. Economic variables interact with social and political issues which are partially unobserved. For instance, if environmental quality is a luxury good, environmental quality is likely to be better in a wealthier country. It is then more likely to reduce deforestation because the amounts and effectiveness of forest protection measures are larger. Then fixed-effect estimators are appropriate and random-effect estimators are inconsistent.[3]

In line with Scrieciu (2007), we think that a lot of previous studies on deforestation drivers have neglected potential autocorrelation issues. We thus test our results for potential existence of autocorrelation by performing Wooldrige's (2002b) test for first-order autocorrelation.[4] In any case, we cannot reject the null hypothesis of no first-order autocorrelation (the probability exceeds 30 percent on average).

We estimate model (4.1) by fixed-effect (FE) and double FE formulations.[5] In the last case, period fixed effects are added to model (4.1) to control the presence of some structural breaks (a global economic crisis, a global drop in timber prices, . . .).[6]

Finally, a heteroskedasticity problem was detected by inspecting the modified Wald test for groupwise heteroskedasticity: the null hypothesis of homoskedasticity[7] is rejected in favor of pairwise heteroskedasticity. However, this result may be interpreted cautiously because the power of this test is low when we regress a fixed-effect model in a context of a short panel. Hence, to check the robustness of our results, we control for heteroskedasticity concerns performing regressions using the correction related to the Eicker–White matrix (see results in Table 4.1).[8]

4.3.2   The unsustainable nature of timber harvesting

Our panel-data analysis is threefold. First, we estimate model (4.1) with our full sample. Second, taking into account the fact that deforestation patterns are difficult to assess for such a heterogeneous panel, we restrict our analysis to developing countries. Finally, to deal with potential outliers in our data, we test our model considering five-year average deforestation rates. Table 4.1 presents results for the harvest-volume variable, while Table 4.2 focuses on the harvest-value variables.

Full-sample analysis

As a first step, our analysis focuses on our whole sample of 87 countries (first two columns of Tables 4.1 and 4.2), to have a global picture of the link between timber harvesting and deforestation.

Overall, the results concerning our control variables are consistent with our expectations and the literature. The weakness of the coefficients is in line with previous empirical studies of deforestation drivers like Nguyen

Table 4.1 Harvest volume and deforestation

	All Countries		Developing countries		
	Annual deforestation		Annual deforestation		5-year average deforestation
	FE	Double FE	FE	Double FE	FE
Harvest-volume	0.006** (2.18)	0.010*** (3.08)	0.006*** (2.67)	0.010*** (3.82)	0.003** (2.46)
Institutions	7.00e-04*** (2.93)	5.00e-04** (2.06)	7.00e-04** (2.25)	5.00e-04* (1.65)	2.00e-04 (0.63)
GDP	1.49e-06** (2.18)	1.93e-06** (2.56)	2.50e-06* (1.69)	2.82e-06* (1.84)	3.89e-06 (1.13)
GDP^2	−3.9e-11** (−2.35)	−3.43e-11* (−1.80)	−7.23e-11 (−0.56)	−5.89e-11 (−0.47)	−2.09e-10 (−0.80)
Growth	−0.01 (−1.14)	−0.01 (−1.54)	−0.01 (−0.95)	−0.02 (−1.34)	−0.01* (−1.81)
Population density	2.05e-05 (1.41)	1.64e-05** (0.95)	3.23e-05 (2.39)	1.24e-05 (0.7)	−9.96e-07 (−0.06)
Forest cover					0.04*** (3.28)
Constant	−0.06** (−2.33)	−0.10*** (−3.22)	−0.06*** (−2.95)	−0.13*** (−4.02)	−0.39*** (−3.66)
DW	2.07	2.09	2.04	2.07	2.02
F-statistic	3.78	3.98	4.21	3.36	2.85
Adj. R^2	0.12	0.13	0.14	0.15	0.31

Note: *, ** and *** indicate significance at the 1%, 5% and 10% level, respectively. Robust t-statistics are in parentheses. The F-statistic is for the significance of country fixed effects in FE regressions or fixed and time effects in Double FE regressions. DW is the Durbin–Watson statistic.

Table 4.2 Harvest value and deforestation

	All Countries		Developing countries		
	Annual deforestation		Annual deforestation		5-year average deforestation
	FE	Double FE	FE	Double FE	FE
Harvest-value	0.002* (1.75)	0.013*** (3.35)	0.002 (1.51)	0.018*** (3.43)	0.002** (1.99)
Institutions	7.00e-04*** (3.05)	4.00e-04 (1.58)	7.00e-04** (2.32)	3.86e-04 (1.09)	3.28e-04 (0.76)
GDP	8.00e-07 (1.23)	4.97e-07 (0.74)	1.03e-06 (0.63)	-2.22e-07 (-0.13)	1.14e-06 (0.31)
GDP^2	-2.5e-11 (-1.57)	5.45e-12 (0.29)	-6.43e-12 (-0.05)	6.15e-11 (0.44)	-4.64e-11 (-0.17)
Growth	-0.006 (-0.59)	-0.01 (-1.31)	-0.007 (-0.54)	-0.01 (-0.87)	-0.01* (-1.65)
Population density	3e-05* (1.74)	2.3e-05 (1.17)	3.65e-05** (2.04)	2.7e-05 (1.54)	2.26e-08 (0.001)
Forest cover					0.04*** (3.08)
Constant	-0.03* (-1.92)	-0.17*** (-3.44)	-0.03* (-1.70)	-0.22*** (-3.49)	-0.38*** (-3.17)
DW	2.05	2.10	2.02	2.07	2.03
F-statistic	3.92	4.63	4.31	3.84	3.15
Adj. R^2	0.12	0.15	0.14	0.18	0.33

Note: *, ** and *** indicate significance at the 1%, 5% and 10% level, respectively. Robust t-statistics are in parentheses. The F-statistic is for the significance of country fixed effects in FE regressions or fixed and time effects in double FE regressions.

Van and Azomahou (2007) or Arcand *et al.* (2008). Moreover, those results are quite robust to the specifications (fixed or double fixed effects) that have been adopted.

Better institutions (low score) tend to be negatively and significantly related to deforestation. We find some evidence of an environmental Kuznets curve when the *Harvest-Volume* variable is used, but not with the *Harvest-Value* variable. Economic growth is negatively related to defor-estation but the coefficients have very low significance. *Population density* is not significantly related to deforestation at a global level except for one regression (*Harvest-Volume* with double fixed effects). Moreover, the coefficients that we found are very weak.

Timber harvesting (both in volume and value) is positively and signif-icantly related to deforestation, both with fixed effects and double fixed effects. We find some evidence that countries relying heavily on timber har-vesting deforest more than countries with smaller timber harvest. One could think that the non-sustainability of timber harvesting is only true in coun-tries with poor institutions and high corruption. Nevertheless, our result holds when controlling for institutional quality. As discussed in Section 4.2, this result needs to be cautiously interpreted: this strong relationship does not necessarily mean that unsustainable forest management is a leading fac-tor of deforestation. Timber harvesting may also come as a by-product of agricultural expansion, which is the main leading factor of deforestation. Nevertheless, in any cases, this result certainly gives the alarming insight that timber harvesting is unsustainable worldwide, even in countries with strong institutions. Indeed, the positive correlation that we find, between timber harvesting and deforestation, shows that timber harvesting builds on the conversion of forests to other land uses.

Can deforestation patterns be identified at a global level? The case of developing countries

As a second step, as mentioned by Scrieciu (2007), the fact that patterns of deforestation are difficult to identify globally is taken into account. Indeed, although we found that our variable of interest is significantly related to deforestation, we also found that fixed effects are very significant (see the F-statistics in Tables 4.1 and 4.2). This large heterogeneity across our sample is likely to decrease the overall significance of our results. Acknowl-edging this fact, we estimate model (4.1), focusing on low-income countries (which corresponds to the sample used by Nguyen Van and Azomahou 2007). Results are given in columns 3 and 4 of Tables 4.1 and 4.2.

Other papers try to overcome this problem of heterogeneity among deforesting countries. Among others, Leplay and Thoyer (2011) choose to distinguish their sample according to the countries forest cover. Culas (2007) splits his sample by continent. We chose to focus on development for two reasons. First, countries experiencing higher deforestation rates are generally developing countries. Second, forest sectors tend to be relatively more important in developing countries. For instance, forest sectors account for 4 percent of GDP in Brazil, 2.5 percent in Indonesia and 4.5 percent in the Central African Republic. In smaller countries, it can go up to 13 percent in Guinea-Bissau, or 9 percent in Chad. In contrast, it accounts for only 1.3 percent in the United States, 0.9 percent in Germany, and 3 percent in Canada (Lebedys 2004).

As expected, the overall significance of our results slightly increases, and is comparable to other studies.[9] Moreover, they are consistent with those derived for the whole sample. The institution variable is significant and the population density is significant under FE methods. In contrast, the growth rate is not significant and we do not find evidence of a Kuznets curve anymore.

Finally, timber harvesting is positively and significantly correlated to deforestation in low-income countries whatever the model estimated. This result makes sense when considering both pressure on the land use and the importance of primary sectors in developing countries.

Dealing with outliers and introducing the impact of the forest cover

As a final step, we test the robustness of our results to the presence of outliers (as mentioned in Section 4.3.1). We proceed as in Combes Motel *et al.* (2009) and compute average deforestation rates over 5-year periods, allowing us to better identify the long-term effects of deforestation drivers and deal with outliers that have previously been suspected.

Moreover, this method allows us to introduce the initial forest cover variable and to test for the forest transition hypothesis. Indeed, we could not assess the role of the initial forest area on deforestation in the previous *within* estimates due to the collinearity (i) between the initial forest cover (i.e. a constant) and the fixed effects;[10] and (ii) between the current forest cover and timber harvest. With our 5-year average, the initial forest cover concerning each period is not correlated with fixed effects anymore because there is sufficient variation within countries.

Column 5 of Tables 4.1 and 4.2 presents our results. Note that only country fixed effects are included since the time dimension is now confined. Overall, the results are very similar to the previous ones, with larger explanatory power. In addition, the magnitude of the coefficients is consistent and the harvest variables are always significant at the 5 percent level. There is nonetheless some divergence: the institution variable is not significant anymore, whereas the growth rate becomes significant at 10 percent. Finally, we find some evidence of a forest transition as the forest cover variable is widely significant.

As a final robustness check, we tested our results using a variable of arable cropland expansion (source: WRI) as a proxy for deforestation, and found similar results (available upon request). However, in this case, autocorrelation has to be cautiously corrected for by Cochrane–Orcutt methodology. Finally, in the next section we test our results in cross-section with more recent deforestation data (2005–10), and also find similar results.

4.4 The influence of timber certification

As shown in Section 4.3, countries with more important forestry sectors and with higher levels of timber production tend to experience higher deforestation rates than others, which gives the insight that timber harvesting tends not to be sustainable. To face this critical concern, timber certification is frequently mentioned as a potential market tool to reduce over-harvesting of forest resources. We present two major timber certification schemes and analyze their relation to deforestation.

4.4.1 Certification schemes and deforestation

Among several certification schemes, we focus on the Forest Stewardship Council (FSC) and the Programme for the Endorsement of Forest Certification (PEFC) schemes (for a complete comparison, see Fischer *et al.* 2005). The FSC scheme covers about 135 million hectares worldwide (data publicly available on FSC website, December 2010), while the PEFC scheme is more important, covering 232 million hectares (data publicly available on PEFC website, December 2010).

While the FSC scheme was initiated by environmental non-governmental organizations in 1993, the PEFC was created in 1999 by European forest owners' associations. The FSC can be considered as a more independent scheme than the PEFC, which is applied by the forest industry itself as a form of self-certification. While both schemes consider environmental, social and economic impacts of timber harvesting,[11] they are likely to follow different kinds of objectives. The PEFC tends to give more voice to business issues, while FSC focuses more on environmental and social issues.

The main difference usually highlighted between both schemes concerns their guidelines, being either performance-based (with outcome requirements) or system-based (with criteria to design forest management for reaching environmental performance). The FSC is essentially a performance-based mechanism, relying on a code of good conduct for forestry operations. A weakness of this scheme is that it has a high level of requirements, which may be taken as a lack of flexibility and limit the access to the scheme for less performing forest managers. In contrast, the PEFC is system-based, with a framework for the development of national or local certification schemes, which may create heterogeneity and inconsistencies in the real quality of PEFC certified products.

Consequently, the FSC scheme is usually considered as more trustworthy concerning environmental quality and sustainable harvesting. For instance, the WWF (in Fischer *et al.* 2005) recommends the use of FSC certification, but not of PEFC certification, because of a lack of transparency and inconsistent quality. The two schemes are thus interesting to compare, since they crucially differ in their implementation and motivations.

Both certification schemes having been created quite recently, it is not possible to implement our panel-data analysis with certification variables. We thus switch to cross-country analysis, since we only have cross-country timber certification data.

We test the following cross-country model:

$$Deforestation_i = \alpha_0 + \alpha_1 Harvest_i + \alpha_2 Certification_i + \alpha_3 H_i + u_i$$

$$(4.2)$$

Our *Deforestation* indicator is the net decrease in forest cover for the period. *Certification* is the proportion of certified forests in the countries considered. We use sequentially the proportion of FSC and PEFC certified forests in 2005 (*FSC, PEFC*; expected sign $-$).

With a view to obtaining comparable results, we use the same set of variables as in the previous section, for the year 2005 (see description in Appendix 4B): institutional quality (*Institutions*),[12] development (*GDP, GDP^2, Growth*), population density (*Population Density*). We also test for the forest transition hypothesis, using the countries' forest cover in 2005 (*Forest Cover*, expected sign $+$). Finally, the two harvest variables are introduced as in the panel analysis (*Harvest-Volume, Harvest-Value*).

4.4.2   Econometric methodology

Model (4.2) is estimated by ordinary least squares. We can expect some endogeneity problems facing reverse causality between the deforestation rate and regressors such as *Forest Cover* and *Harvest-Volume*.

We controlled for endogeneity using the Hausman (1978) test, and we reject the presence of endogeneity. However, considering our database, those results should be interpreted cautiously because the inability of the Hausman test to identify endogeneity is likely to reflect the small sample size. Thus, we choose variables refereing to the beginning of the overall period (2005).

In addition, we control for heteroskedasticity concerns by performing regressions using White heteroskedasticity-consistent standard errors and covariance. Multicollinearity is ruled out through the variance inflation factor.

4.4.3 Timber certification as a sustainability indicator

Our results are given in Table 4.3.[13] The introduction of our certification variable induces some changes in our set of control variables. Better institutional quality (lower index) is negatively related to deforestation (although we find less significant coefficients than in the panel-data case). There is no strong evidence of an environmental Kuznets curve for deforestation (the coefficient has the expected sign only when considering the PEFC scheme). Population density is strongly and positively related to deforestation for the FSC case, while it is not significant in the PEFC case. This may be because of the geographical prevalence of the certification schemes: the FSC is relatively more represented in tropical and developing countries than the PEFC. Our results only partially support the idea of a forest transition: the initial forest cover is only significantly and positively related to deforestation in the PEFC case.

The area of FSC certified forests is strongly and negatively related to deforestation. The value of the coefficients is stable whatever our specification. Moreover, we note that our harvest indicators are not significant anymore (while they are significant when *FSC* and *PEFC* are not considered). Countries that rely heavily on timber certification tend to experience sustainable timber harvesting.

Analyzing the relation between PEFC and deforestation provides contrasted results. Indeed, the area of PEFC certified forest is not related to deforestation when considering our *Harvest-Volume* variable. Moreover, the harvest variable is significatively and positively related to deforestation in this case. In contrast, when considering the *Harvest-Value* variable, our PEFC indicator is negatively and strongly related to deforestation. This means that PEFC can be considered as a reliable sustainability indicator only when prices are taken into account. Indeed, certification usually tends to increase timber prices. Ozanne and Vlosky (1997) report that consumers are willing to pay a maximum 50 percent price premium for certified forest products (Fischer *et al.* 2005). Those higher prices can in this context be considered as incentives for sustainable forest management.

Table 4.3 Timber certification and deforestation

	FSC volume	FSC value	PEFC volume	PEFC value
FSC	−0.12**	−0.12*		
	(−2.17)	(−1.80)		
PEFC			0.01	−0.14**
			(1.07)	(−2.52)
Harvest-volume	0.002		0.01**	
	(0.31)		(2.53)	
Harvest-value		−0.006		0.01
		(−0.62)		(1.51)
GDP	−7.79e-06**	−9.18e-06**	5.07e-06	4.31e-06
	(−2.48)	(−2.61)	(1.62)	(1.28)
GDP^2	8.27e-11	1.08e-10	−1.11e-10**	−1.03e-10*
	(1.39)	(1.52)	(−2.01)	(−1.78)
Growth	−0.02**	−0.02**	−0.011**	−0.009
	(−2.26)	(−2.63)	(−2.13)	(−1.56)
Population density	1.32e-05***	1.41e-05***	−8.34e-05	−3.29e-06
	(2.90)	(3.02)	(−0.79)	(−0.02)
Institutions	0.007∗	0.008∗	0.003	0.002
	(1.74)	(1.70)	(1.11)	(0.63)
Forest cover	−0.004	−0.002	0.03***	0.01***
	(−0.50)	(−0.24)	(4.37)	(4.73)
Constant	0.20	0.31	−0.51***	−0.55***
	(1.06)	(1.47)	(−4.03)	(−3.08)
Adjusted R^2	0.39	0.41	0.64	0.70

Robust *t*-statistics are in parentheses;
Results using White heteroskedasticity-consistent standard errors and covariance.
*10% level of significance; **5% level of significance; ***1% level of significance.

We should, however, repeat that results need to be cautiously interpreted because the number of observations is quite low. Moreover the
PEFC certification is essentially present in developed countries, for which
deforestation is less important than for developing countries.

4.5   Conclusion

Our panel-data analysis gives some evidence that timber harvesting is positively related to deforestation. This strong relationship implies that demand
for timber products is to a large extent fulfilled by unsustainable timber
harvesting: harvested timber comes either as a by-product of agricultural
expansion, or from unsustainable forest management leading to land-use
change. Our results hold for the whole set of countries, but are stronger
when focusing on low-income countries and considering outliers.

A potential consequence in the long run, and considering the projected increase in demand for timber products, is that timber prices will increase significantly, as forests become a scarcer resource. We also show that a price effect tends to exacerbate this relation. Then this unsustainable nature of timber harvesting would be self-enhancing: forest scarcity increases timber prices, and timber prices are positively correlated to deforestation, which would increase timber scarcity.

Our results hold when considering the quality of countries' institutions: timber harvesting is positively correlated with deforestation even in countries with reliable institutions and low levels of corruption. However, if global institutional quality does not seem to prevent unsustainable timber harvesting, strengthening institutions specifically related to forests, like reliable forest certification, tends to weaken this pernicious relationship. Indeed, timber certification appears to be related to sustainable forest management (negatively related to deforestation), which gives support to organizations militating for the boycott and banning of non-certified timber (Chapter 6, this volume). It is worthwhile noting that this result is stronger when considering more demanding certification schemes. This result raises the question of the motivations behind environmental certification schemes (Bottega *et al.* 2009). When market-based motives come along with environmental motives, the resulting certification scheme may not be demanding enough to efficiently prevent forest depletion.

Certification may have a direct and an indirect impact on unsustainable timber harvesting. First, by imposing codes of good practice, it can directly increase forest management sustainability. Second, certified timber is usually sold at higher prices. Then, if those higher prices increase the marginal value given to forests, certification may offset the pressures for agricultural expansion and indirectly reduce deforestation.

In this context, it thus appears important to help developing certification schemes in developing countries. As noticed in Fischer *et al.* (2005), several barriers limit the adoption of certification in the developing world, such as high certification costs, limited local willingness to pay for environmentally friendly goods, lack of information and political support. It then appears important to work on reducing those barriers and facilitate certification adoption in the developing world.

Finally, as noticed by Scrieciu (2007), the high significance of fixed effects underlines the difficulty of assessing the deforestation patterns at a global level. This crucial statement opens up an important field of future research, which is to investigate the sources of divergence and heterogeneity between countries experiencing high deforestation rates.

Appendix 4A: Panel 1972–94 database description

Table 4.4 Country list

Algeria	Costa Rica	Jamaica	Paraguay	Australia	Japan
Argentina	Dominican Republic	Jordan	Peru	Austria	Norway
Argentina	Ecuador	Kenya	Philippines	Bulgaria	New Zealand
Bangladesh	Egypt	Korea, South	Rwanda	Canada	Poland
Benin	El Salvador	Madagascar	Senegal	Germany	Portugal
Brazil	Fiji	Malawi	Singapore	Denmark	Romania
Burkina Faso	Gambia	Malaysia	Sri Lanka	Spain	Saudi Arabia
Burundi	Ghana	Mali	Syria	Finland	Sweden
Cameroon	Guatemala	Mauritius	Thailand	France	Switzerland
Central African Republic	Guyana	Mexico	Togo	UK	USA
Chile	Haiti	Morocco	Trinidad & Tobago	Greece	
China	Honduras	Nicaragua	Tunisia	Hungaria	
Colombia	India	Niger	Turkey	Ireland	
Congo, Rep.	Indonesia	Pakistan	Uruguay	Iceland	
Congo. Dem. Rep.	Ivory Coast	Panama	Venezuela	Israel	
			Zambia	Italy	

Table 4.5 Descriptive statistics for all countries

Variables	Mean	Standard deviation	Min	Max
Deforestation rate	0.002	0.018	−0.280	0.228
Roundwood harvest volume	27,236.25	65,929.27	0	513,000
Average timber price	39.662	23.224	11.552	262.559
Civil liberties	3.713	1.876	1	7
Political rights	3.679	2.197	1	7
Institutions	6.461	2.570	2	14
GDP	4,228.279	6,363.040	330.368	27,877.940
Growth	0.014	0.047	−0.286	0.236
Population density	91.991	119.697	1.7	964.7

Table 4.6 Descriptive statistics for high-income countries

Variable	Mean	Standard deviation	Min	Max
Deforestation rate	0.0022	0.014	−0.138	0.14
Roundwood	41,410	91,847	0	513,000
Average price	55.5	25.9	13.1	262.6
Institutions	3.01	3.80	2	12
GDP	16,088.7	4,381.9	5,616.6	27,877.9
Growth	2.0	3.3	−16.3	21.4
Population density	95.2	82.2	1.7	342.7
Real exchange rate	105.4	28.4	42.3	281.0
Arable land	19,001	40,337	384	190,624
Initial forest cover	49,804	110,614	106	453,300
Exports	2,398,984	3,714,368	17,264	21,995,093

Table 4.7 Descriptive statistics for low-income countries

Variable	Mean	Standard deviation	Min	Max
Deforestation rate	0.002	0.018	−0.184	0.228
Roundwood	19,052	46,411	14	312,788
Average price	28.6	9.82	11.6	63.0
Institutions	8.75	3.28	2	14
GDP	3,437.8	2,693.1	330.4	21,249.8
Growth	0.89	5.23	−28.60	23.60
Population density	92.5	135.2	3.1	964.7
Real exchange rate	141.9	58.4	30.3	478.3

Table 4.7 Continued

Variable	Mean	Standard deviation	Min	Max
Arable land	8,874	23,008	2	169,790
Initial forest cover	28,971.1	77,191.6	5	563,911.0
Exports	194,713.4	417,594.8	0	2,652,088

Table 4.8 Variable description

Variable	Definition	Source
Deforestation	Yearly percentage of variation of the forest cover	FAO
Harvest volume	Log of the volume of roundwood harvested	FAO
Average timber price	Yearly average price of timber	FAO
Harvest value	*Harvest volume* times *Average timber price*	
Civil liberties	"Freedoms to develop views, institutions, and personal autonomy apart from state", index from 1 (high) to 7 (low)	Freedom House
Political rights	"Permitting people to freely take part in the political process that represents the method by which the policymakers are chosen to make effective decisions, index from 1 (high) to 7 (low)	Freedom House
Institutions	Sum of *Civil liberties* and *Political rights*	
GDP	Gross domestic product per capita	Penn World Table 6.1
Growth	Annual percentage growth rate of GDP at market prices based on constant local currency	World bank tables
Population density	People per squared kilometer	World Bank tables
Forest cover	Percentage of land covered by forests	FAO
Exports	Log of exports in forest products (thousands of dollars)	World Resource Institute
Arable land	Log of arable land expansion (hectares)	World Resource Institute

Appendix 4B: Cross-section database description

Table 4.9 PEFC country list

Australia	Austria	Belgium	Brazil	Canada	Chile
China	Colombia	Czechoslovakia	Denmark	Egypt	Estonia
Finland	France	Germany	Hungary	India	Indonesia
Ireland	Italy	Japan	Korea, South	Latvia	Lithuania
Luxembourg	Malaysia	Mexico	Morocco	Netherlands	New Zealand
Norway	Peru	Poland	Portugal	Puerto Rico	Romania
Singapore	Slovak Republic	Slovenia	South Africa	Spain	Sweden
Switzerland	Thailand	Tunisia	Turkey	UK	USA
United Arab Emirates					

Table 4.10 FSC country list

Argentina	Australia	Austria	Belarus	Belgium	Belize
Bolivia	Brazil	Canada	Chile	China	Colombia
Costa Rica	Croatia	Czechoslovakia	Denmark	Ecuador	Estonia
Finland	France	Germany	Greece	Guatemala	Honduras
Hungary	Indonesia	Ireland	Italy	Japan	Kenya
Latvia	Lithuania	Malaysia	Mexico	Namibia	Nepal
Netherlands	New Zealand	Nicaragua	Panama	Papua New Guinea	Paraguay
Peru	Poland	Romania	Slovak Republic	Solomon Island	South Africa
Spain	Sri Lanka	Swaziland	Sweden	Switzerland	UK
USA	USSR	Uganda	Ukraine	Uruguay	Zimbabwe

Table 4.11 Certification variable description

Variable	Definition	Source
FSC	Proportion of FSC certified forest area in 2005	UNEP
PEFC	Proportion of PEFC certified forest area in 2005	PEFC

Table 4.12 Descriptive statistics

Variable	Mean	Standard deviation	Min	Max
Deforestation	−0.075	0.086	−0.258	0.217
Harvest-Volume	29,088	69,962	0	471,862
Price	58.45	29.70	30.96	169.41
FSC (ha)	942,376	2,170,710	56	10,400,300
PEFC (ha)	5,036,715	18,626,089	0	1.19 E08
Institutions	5.73	3.53	2	14
GDP	12,296	12,693	185	47,305
Growth	0.045	0.026	−0.053	0.10
Population Density	332.28	1,352.06	2.65	10,818.30
Forest Cover (ha)	45,152,899	1.23 e08	46,000	8.09 e08

References

Amacher, G. S. (2006) Corruption: A challenge for economists interested in forest policy design. *Journal of Forest Economics*, 12(2): 85–9.

Angelsen, A. and Kaimowitz, D. (1999) Rethinking the causes of deforestation: Lessons from economic models. *World Bank Research Observer*, 14(1): 73–98.

Arcand, J.-L., Guillaumont, P. and Jeanneney-Guillaumont, S. (2008) Deforestation and the real exchange rate. *Journal of Development Economics*, 86(2): 242–62.

Bhattarai, M. and Hammig, M. (2001) Institutions and the environmental Kuznets curve for deforestation: A crosscountry analysis for Latin America, Africa and Asia. *World Development*, 29(6): 995–1010.

Bottega, L., Delacote, P. and Ibanez, L. (2009) Labeling policies and market behavior: Quality standard and voluntary label adoption. *Journal of Agricultural & Food Industrial Organization*, 7(2).

Combes Motel, P., Pirard, R. and Combes, J.-L. (2009) A methodology to estimate impacts of do- mestic policies on deforestation: Compensated successful efforts for avoided deforestation (REDD). *Ecological Economics*, 68(3): 680–91.

Culas, R. J. (2007) Deforestation and the environmental Kuznets curve: An institutional perspective. *Ecological Economics*, 61(2–3): 429–37.

Drukker, D. (2003) Testing for serial correlation in linear panel-data models. *Stata Journal*, 3(2): 168–177.

Ewers, R. M. (2006) Interaction effects between economic development and forest cover determine deforestation rates. *Global Environmental Change*, 16: 161–169.

FAO (2009) State of the world forests. Technical report, FAO, Rome.

FAO (2010) State of the world forests. Technical report, FAO, Rome.

Fischer, C., Sedjo, R., Jawahar, P. and Aguilar, F. (2005) Forest certification: Toward common standards? Discussion Papers dp-05-10, Resources For the Future.

Hausman, J. (1978) Specification tests in econometrics. *Econometrica*, 46(6): 1251–72.

Hsiao, C. (1986) *Analysis of Panel Data*. Cambridge: Cambridge University Press.

Kaufmann, D., Kaay, A. and Mastruzzi, M. (2008) Governance matter vii: Aggregate and individual governance indicators 1996–2007. Policy Research Working Paper, World Bank.

Lebedys, A. (2004) Trends and current status of the contribution of the forestry sector to national economies. FAO Working paper FSFM/ACC/07.

Leplay, S. and Thoyer, S. (2011) Synergy effects of international policy instruments to reduce deforestation: a cross-country panel data analysis. LAMETA Working Paper, 2011-01.

Mayer, P. (2000) Hot spot: Forest policy in europe: achievements of the MCPFE and challenges ahead. *Forest Policy and Economics*, 1(2): 177–85.

Nguyen Van, P. and Azomahou, T. (2007) Nonlinearities and heterogeneity in environmental quality: An empirical analysis of deforestation. *Journal of Development Economics*, 84(1): 291–309.

Ozanne, L. and Vlosky, R. (1997) Environmental certification of wood products. *Women in Natural Resources*, 19(3): 4–8.

Roodman, D. (2009) How to do xtabond2: An introduction to difference and system GMM in Stata. *Stata Journal*, 9 (1): 86–136.

Rudel, T. K., Coomes, O. T., Moran, E., Achard, F., Angelsen, A., Xu, J. and Lambin, E. (2005) Forest transitions: Towards a global understanding of land use change. *Global Environmental Change Part A*, 15(1): 23–31.

Scrieciu, S. S. (2007) Can economic causes of tropical deforestation be identified at a global level? *Ecological Economics*, 62(3–4): 603–12.

UNEP (2003) Les forêts. In *Geo 2003*. Nairobi: UNEP.

White, H. (1980) A heteroskedasticity-consistent covariance matrix and direct test for het-eroskedasticity. *Econometrica*, 48(4): 817–38.

Wooldridge, J. (2002a) *Econometric Analysis of Cross Section and Panel Data*. Cambridge, MA: MIT Press.

Wooldridge, J. (2002b) *Introductory Econometrics. A Modern Approach*. Cincinnati, OH: South-Western College Publishers.

Part IV
Global
Citizen consumption

5 Political consumerism and public policy
Good complements against market failures?

This chapter was written with Claire Montagné (INRA-AgroParisTech, Laboratory of Forest Economics) and published in *Ecological Economics* 73 (2011).

5.1 Introduction

> My dream would be to see an emerging movement of citizen consumers, driven by the youth and refusing every carbon-consuming product. It is the only thing that could make multinational firms and governments radically change trajectory. Everyone should do their own carbon assessment.
>
> (Pachauri 2008; author's translation)

According to Rajendra Pachauri (2008), the solution to global warming – and potentially other global environmental concerns – could only result from individuals' mobilization through voluntary actions as responsible international citizens. The citizen consumer mentioned by Pachauri relies on "consumption practices aimed at engaging the citizens' moral responsibility and taking into account social and environmental criteria in the purchase process according to the sustainable development principle" (Mylondo 2005). It thus refers to consumers' preferences towards goods and services with social and environmental production and distribution conditions that are consistent with sustainability (Begaudin and Demontrand 2007; Ferrando y Puig and Giamporcaro-Saunière 2005). The literature gives different terms for this citizen engagement of consumers in the economic sphere such as: citizen, ethical, green, sustainable, or socially conscious consumerism (Theron 2010). In this study, we use the more encompassing term of "political consumerism", defined by Micheletti *et al.*

(2004) as "consumer choice of producers and products on the basis of attitudes and values that concern issues of personal and family well-being as well as ethical and political assessment of favorable and unfavorable business and government practice." Political consumerism entails the use of the market as an arena for politics where consumers bring their political concerns, using the power of their individual choice to protest against institutional practices that are objectionable (Micheletti and Stolle 2008). Such a political consumerism may be seen as forms of "conceptual consumption" in which people consume concepts – environmental quality, health, social well being, social status, etc. – rather than the good itself (Ariely and Norton 2009).

Political consumerism has been studied from a large multidisciplinary field: political scientists have been considering political consumerism as a particular variant of political participation; studies in psychology and marketing have focused on the characteristics and motives of citizen consumers (e.g. Jensen 2005; Spangenberg and Lorek 2002; Welsch and Kühling 2009; Baek 2010; Cogoy 1999); economists have analyzed political consumerism as replacement for conventional political participation, such as voting (e.g. Micheletti 2002; Strømsnes 2009), have analyzed the different forms of political consumerism (e.g. Charles 2009; Innes 2006; Nielson 2010), and have described the possible instruments for developing such responsible behaviors (e.g. Coad *et al.* 2009; Schumacher 2010). To our knowledge, Brennan (2006) was the first to analyze a particular form of political consumerism – green preferences – and the related change in consumer preferences, as a possible substitute for traditional policies.

The aim of this chapter is to investigate to what extent political consumerism may represent an effective and fair instrument against environmental and social damages related to consumption, and to what extent it can impact the effectiveness of public policies. Section 5.2 replaces the concept of political consumerism in the context of economic theory. Section 5.3 focuses on political consumerism weaknesses, while Section 5.4 shows how political consumerism can turn into a potentially suitable complement to public policies. Section 5.5 concludes.

5.2   Political consumerism in the light of economic theory

In neoclassical economics, environmental and social damages are the consequences of market failures: resources are misallocated because of non-existent property rights or externalities. Pollution is a negative externality, that is, a by-product of production or consumption. This by-product is indirect, concerning other agents than the one carrying out the activity. Thus, it represents a social cost not taken into account through price mechanisms, which only consider private costs. This externality brings an over-provision of pollution, which is suboptimal in terms of global welfare (Bishop 2004). A variation of this view is that economic theory only assesses "self-regarding" preferences of agents when only "society-regarding" or citizen preferences are appropriate to handle environmental and social issues. In this context, a political consumer may be seen as a person who acts in a socially responsible manner through the market, integrating in his/her consumption behavior other moral, social and ethical aspects of human behaviors (Sagoff 1988; Etzioni 1988). Political consumerism unambiguously represents a decentralized and voluntary response to negative externalities. Through consciously purchasing certain products, it contributes to the redistribution of resources, be it through donations from corporations, empowerment through fair trade or reinforcing ethical values (Theron 2010).

From our point of view, political consumerism may be interpreted as a way in which consumers internalize part of externalities. This form of self-internalization may be expressed as follows. Consider a self-interested consumer with a willingness to pay for a product inducing a negative environmental externality. This willingness to pay results in a downward sloping "selfish" demand function $D(P)$. Consider now the same consumer, who now has some environmental motivations. Those environmental preferences are likely to be expressed by a smaller willingness to pay for the good, resulting in a downward shift of the "selfish" demand function to the "political" demand function $D_c(P) < D(P)$. The extent of political consumerism may be expressed as the difference between the selfish and the political demand.

Two kinds of political consumerism may be distinguished (Micheletti 2003; Strømsnes 2009; Holzer 2006). First, the *boycott* is the negative version of political consumerism, where consumers refrain from buying certain brands or products as a protest against a company or a country's practices. Boycotts can be considered as situations in which the political component of the demand function is larger than the selfish demand function: $D_c(P) < 0$. In this case, the consumer prefers not to consume the good considered, to protest against the firms' practices. Note that in this case, the price premium related to environmental quality encompasses the potential benefit of seeing the targeted firm changes its behavior. Second, the *buycott* is a positive political choice where consumers decide to buy products compatible with their political, ethical or environmental preferences – it includes notably social and environmental certification, and ecolabeling. In our context, a buycott can be defined as a situation in which a non-polluting substitute exists on the market. In this case, the difference between the political demand function $D_c(P)$ and the selfish demand function $D(P)$ is explained by the fact that consumers switch a part of their consumption from the polluting good to the clean substitute. A better, cleaner and cheaper substitute is then likely to increase the extent of political consumerism.

While boycotts aim to punish firms or countries for irresponsible behaviors, buycotts reward firms for virtuous ones (Friedman 1996). Data from the European Social Survey 2002–2003 (http://www.european-socialsurvey.org/) indicate that 35 percent of respondents in Europe are political consumers; 13 percent of those boycott, 46 percent buycott, and 41 percent both boycott and buycott (Nielson 2010). From this point of view, one may thus wonder whether political consumerism is an efficient instrument against market failures such as externalities, in the context of public policies.

5.3   Political consumerism against market failures?

As shown before, political consumerism may be seen as a way for consumers to self-internalize externalities such as pollution and other environmental damages. Is this type of internalization efficient? Can it be a good substitute for other types of internalization or is it a fair complement to them? We first focus on some weaknesses of political consumerism, which may prevent it from being an effective instrument to internalize externalities.

5.3.1   Is political consumerism a good indicator of the social cost of environmental degradation?

A crucial limitation of political consumption is the analogy made between consumers and citizens. Indeed, the self-internalization implied by political consumerism may not be efficient if the preferences of the consumers do not match those of the entire community. In other words, is the self-internalization of externalities a good indicator of the social cost of those externalities? Let us define $D^*(P)$ as the optimal demand function that fully integrates the social cost of consuming the polluting good. Then political consumerism represents a fair and effective instrument if $D_c(P)$ gets close enough to $D^*(P)$.

In the context of global issues – global warming, biodiversity losses, etc. – most concerned citizens are not necessarily consumers. In this context, do non-directly concerned consumers have the same preferences as directly concerned ones? For instance, consumers' practices are an important vector of global warming; however, consumers are to a large extent very different from the main global warming victims. In a few words, industrialized countries – and their consumers – are to a large extent responsible of global warming, while the main victims are among people from the developing South. Northern consumers may not feel the same sense urgency as Southern victims. Therefore, even if partially integrated in their preferences, the global cost perceived by Northern citizens may be smaller than the overall social cost of global warming.

This analogy between consumers and citizens is thus quite questionable in terms of fairness. There is no guarantee that consumers' preferences are representative of the whole community preferences. Many concerned citizens – from the developing South – are mainly outside the market or are of little economic importance. Political consumerism in this sense raises the problem of excluding the market from democratic systems of legitimation (Baldwin 2008). Putting too much confidence in political consumption would thus consist in introducing a political decision bias, creating what could be called a "consumarchy", in which richer consumers would have more influence than poorer citizens. In this sense, it could appear as very restrictive to confound market power and political power.

5.3.2 *Collective limitation of individual actions*

To have an effective macroeconomic impact, political consumerism needs to be of large enough scale, in order to properly shape the market outcome. This scale depends essentially on the coordination of individual actions. Individual consumers usually have marginal market influence, which implies that collective action must emerge in order to have significant impact. However, consumers are generally poorly integrated, and thus are likely to be concerned by usual problem of collective action (see Chapter 6, this volume). Indeed, political consumerism is costly, both in terms of learning and information acquiring (Which cleaner substitute should I consume? Where can it be found?) and in terms of monetary or opportunity costs (How good is this clean substitute compared to the polluting one? How much am I ready to pay for it?).

Individual consumers thus have to trade off a costly action against its small positive impact. If each individual takes this tradeoff into consideration, we are in the usual coordination problem of the voter's paradox (Downs 1957): a costly action with virtually no marginal impact. Moreover, consumers may be reluctant to make efforts and reduce their polluting consumption, if they are only a few to do so. In this case, nobody wants to get the "sucker's payoff" (Bougherara *et al.* 2009), and participation in political consumerism is low. This tradeoff seems to be even stronger in situations in which tipping points are crucial (e.g. climate change, where the marginal low impact of one's individual behavior is exacerbated.

Moreover, individual consumption behaviors are largely anonymous, and there is no real social control of consumption. Thus, even environmentally sensitive consumers have an incentive to free-ride. Even if preferring the emergence of green consumption at a global scale, individual consumers are confronted with the usual prisoner's dilemma: for example, global green consumption could be an optimal situation, but individually, green consumption is strictly dominated by regular consumption. This effect is important here especially because of the atomicity of individual consumers. In other words, why would I invest in costly actions with small marginal impact if nobody does the same? In this case, as argued by Howley *et al.* (2010), "individuals express different preferences when adopting collective as opposed to personal choices". In this sense, consumption patterns are not a good indicator of environmental and social preferences, and $D_c(P)$ gets farther away from $D^*(P)$.

The lack of coordination and free-riding issues may thus considerably decrease the influence of political consumerism. Even if consumers have strong environmental preferences, they are likely to be discouraged by the cost of political consumption and by its relatively marginal impact. Therefore, the large coordination and information campaigns that are nowadays launched via social networks help reduce this weakness.

5.3.3 Information and shaping of public opinion

Another crucial weakness of political consumerism may thus arise from the fact that consumers may not be sufficiently and correctly informed, which has two main consequences.

First, the choice of the issues may be directly influenced by mass media or non-governmental organizations (NGOs). In summary, a good news subject is not necessarily crucial in terms of social welfare. Indeed, the choice process of issues covered may not be directed by social welfare considerations. In contrast, issues may be selected because they are spectacular or because they can mobilize public opinion. For example, with regard to the Brent Spar case, Greenpeace admitted in September 2005 inaccurate claims that Spar contained 5,500 tonnes of oil and apologized to Shell. In this case, mass media widely covered the event, helping to create an important event out of inaccurate information.

Second, consumers may be imperfectly informed of the actual environmental quality of the good they consume. As mentioned before, the temptation to "greenwash" is high if consumers do not have clear information about the good's characteristics. This is precisely the role of certification – to provide information about (unobservable) credence good characteristics. However, even certification schemes may be impenetrable to consumers. Indeed, consumers usually do not know about the real quality behind environmental-friendly or fair-trade goods. They just know that the certified good is somehow better than the regular one, but have no idea of the extent of the improvement. For example, some cosmetics firms provide goods using forest products provided by the Kayapo, an indigenous nation inhabiting the southern part of the Amazon forest. This project is integrated more generally in a "trade not aid" approach: helping poorer people to develop instead of waiting for public aid. However, it has been claimed that the Kayapo do not benefit much from this program and that the real importance of their participation in the production process is relatively marginal (Turner 1995).

Effective political consumerism requires transparent and trustworthy information. Conversely, the continuous flow of information may be a source of confusion. Moreover, some actors – firms, NGOs, governments – may be tempted to manipulate available information and bias the consumer's point of view. It appears that those informational issues create important transaction costs that decrease the efficiency of political consumerism.

Overall, it seems that political consumerism is too weak an instrument to efficiently deal with global concerns.

5.4 Political consumerism and public policies

From this point of view, it is possible to consider the implications of political consumerism in the light of public policies. Three types of solution to market failures of this kind may be distinguished (Börkey *et al.* 2000). First, environmental or Pigouvian taxation (Pigou 1920/2002) constitutes a coercive but market-based way to internalize negative externalities. Second, regulatory instruments – standards, quotas, product bans, cap and trade – consist of mandatory environmental performance levels imposed by public authorities. Third, voluntary approaches consist of firms committing to improve their environmental performance. Voluntary approaches may take the form of unilateral commitments made by polluters – such as changes in technologies of production or in consumers' preferences. More frequently, they come from agreements and bargaining between polluters and actors affected by pollution – through the actions of NGOs, public authorities, and individuals.

The options for dealing with externalities are thus numerous, and often depend on the characteristics of the externality. The key is to identify the particular tool or policy alternative that will best move the market towards the most efficient allocation of resources. An important part of the environmental economics literature deals with this optimal design of environmental policy. Several authors consider the different solutions as alternatives and compare them in terms of relative efficiency or equity (e.g. Charles 2009; Fitoussi *et al.* 2007; Grolleau *et al.* 2004; Chiroleu-Assouline 2007; Conrad 2001; Wu 1999; Riera *et al.* 2007), while others try to combine them in a policy mix (e.g. Lee and Yik 2004; Johannsen 2002; OECD 2003; Braathen 2005). We consider here potential synergies and complementarities between political consumerism and public policies.

Examples of environmental public policies

Taxes are used for the regulation of a wide range of environmental concerns. Sweden has been a leading example of the use of energy taxes and specifically a carbon tax. In 1991, the Swedish government restructured the country's tax system by introducing a carbon tax, a value-added tax on energy consumption, and reduced general energy taxes by approximately 50 percent. The carbon tax was set at US$150 per ton of carbon. As a consequence, Swedish emissions have been reduced by 9 percent in the period 1990–2006 and Swedish people are using biomass more and more as an alternative to coal and oil (Johansson 2000).

With the *cap and trade* approach, the regulator sets a cap on emissions of a particular pollutant from a designated group of polluters, divided into individual and tradable permits. A successful example of cap and trade is the Acid Rain Program implemented by the United States Environmental Protection Agency in 1995. This program created one of the first market-based cap and trade mechanisms in the country. It has been and continues to be a great success, and has been a major influence in lowering the annual SO_2 emissions from 17.3 million tons in 1980 to an estimated 8.95 million tons in 2010 (http://www.epa.gov/airmarkets/progsregs/arp/index.html).

Private or public information programs could also contribute to the reduction of market failure. In Sacramento, for example, if people use less energy than their neighbors, they get a smiley face on their utility bill (or two for really efficient energy consumption) – a tactic that has helped reduce energy use in the district and is now being employed in Chicago, Seattle, and eight other US cities (Ariely and Norton 2009).

5.4.1　Environmental taxation

The European Commission (2007) considers market-based and mandatory instruments such as environmental taxation as key instruments in controlling environmental degradation and climate change. Indeed, following Pigou (1920/2002), environmental taxation (or equivalently, subsidy) is a major policy tool for internalizing the social cost of polluting activities. Moreover, Pigouvian taxation is a potentially efficient way in which governments may increase the influence of political consumerism (Schumacher 2010) and vice versa (Coad *et al.* 2009; Buenstorf and Cordes 2008; Linott 1998).

Going back to the simple framework given in Section 5.2, let us assume that a tax is implemented on the polluting good, increasing its price from P to $P + t$. Then the selfish demand curve becomes $D(P + t)$ and the political demand function becomes $D_c(P + t)$. Environmental taxation increases the impact of political consumerism if $-dD_c(P)/dP > -dD(P)/dP$. Indeed, if the political demand curve is more sensitive to prices than the selfish demand curve, political consumerism and environmental taxation are complements.

First, environmental taxation may facilitate the switching of consumption from the polluting good to the clean good, which would support the idea of complementarity. Indeed, environmental taxation reduces the premium that consumers have to pay for environmentally friendly goods. By increasing the price of polluting goods (taxation) and eventually by decreasing the price of clean goods (subsidy), it is clear that taxation may have a great impact in reducing the cost of political consumption. In particular, Schumacher (2010) shows that a subsidy (tax) on the price of an ecolabeled (dirty) good leads to a larger consumption of the ecolabeled (dirty) good, while it decreases the demand for the dirty (ecolabeled) good, if both goods are gross substitutes.

Second, environmental taxation may increase the likelihood of a successful boycott. Indeed, $D_c(P + t)$ has a higher chance of being negative than $D_c(P)$. The action of boycotting implies the opportunity cost of not consuming some good. A tax on the price of this good naturally decreases the consumer surplus of the non-boycotting situation, decreasing thus the opportunity cost of boycotting. Similarly a subsidy on clean substitutes also decreases the cost of boycotting, by increasing the surplus derived from the consumption of the substitute (Chapter 6, this volume).

Third, Coad *et al.* (2009) state that financial incentives alone do not improve the understanding of the problem society faces: individuals view the environment as the responsibility of the government rather than as their own cause. In consequence, it has been empirically observed that the use of financial incentives alone – without due regard for political consumers' preferences – increases the risk of reducing voluntary actions and cooperative intentions. In this case, if, when facing a tax, politically motivated consumers no longer reduced purchases on their own, political consumerism and the tax would be substitutes – which corresponds to the case in which $-dD_c(P)/dP < -dD(P)/dP$.

Finally, it is important to note that political consumerism may blur the environmental taxation design. Indeed, an environmental tax is supposed to match the firm's private cost and the social cost. If consumers already integrate a part of the social cost of pollution into their demand function, the rate of taxation should be lower than if they have a purely selfish demand function. Then, if the policy-maker improperly takes into account the incidence of political consumerism, it is likely to miss the optimal level of taxation. For instance, if the policy-maker takes the apparent demand function into account for setting the environmental tax, it is likely to overshoot the policy. In contrast, it is difficult to estimate the real "selfish" demand function that we defined earlier. Overall, the cost of implementing the right tax may be increasing in situations in which political consumerism is not well known, making it a substitute for political consumerism. As a corollary, environmental taxation is more desirable in situations in which political consumerism is not very developed, or if the nature of political consumerism is well known, making it a good complement for political consumerism.

5.4.2   *Quotas and tradable permits*

Under quotas and tradable permits, the policy-maker sets the socially optimal level of environmental degradation and allocates it to firms. Then, a market for permits is supposed to efficiently allocate the rights to pollute among firms on the market: efficient firms will reduce their pollution and sell their pollution permits to less efficient firms. Note first that political consumerism has no impact on the overall level of pollution. There is then a guarantee that the socially optimal level of pollution will be achieved – as long as it has been properly set by the policy-maker. It follows that a cap and trade system may be desirable if the extent of political consumerism is not well known, so that setting the right environmental tax gets more difficult.

Political consumerism will influence the *ex post* allocation of pollution permits among firms. Since it can be defined as a price premium given to clean firms, the most efficient firms will tend to have some double dividend from this type of policy: they can first benefit from the green consumer's price premium, and then benefit from selling their pollution permits on the market. It follows that political consumerism rewards the most efficient firms and gives an incentive to improve environmental efficiency.

However, if political consumerism is important enough, the permit price on the market is likely to be quite low. In this case, less efficient firm will have little incentive to become more environmentally friendly, since they buy permits at a low market price.

In the case of tradable permits, political consumerism (1) does not impact the overall level of pollution, (2) induces a double dividend for virtuous firms (from the green price premium and selling the permits), but (3) decreases the permit price which may create a pernicious incentive for dirty firms not to improve their environmental efficiency. It is worth noting that political consumers may be opposed to such a policy, if they realize that green consumption and the cap and trade mechanism may indirectly increase pollution from dirty competitors. In this context, lobbies from dirty industries and from green consumption may both oppose cap and trade programs.

5.4.3 Informational programs and voluntary programs

Informational and voluntary programs may enhance the influence of political consumerism on the market outcomes. Indeed, some market characteristics are crucial to success, by increasing the effectiveness of political consumerism, decreasing $D_c(P)$.

First, the emergence of certification and green labeling constitutes a market diversification (Schumacher 2010). Thus, barriers to entry constitute a potential limitation to political consumerism. Indeed, it is clear that if a firm using a polluting technology is in a monopoly position, it is more costly to consumers to fully integrate the social cost of pollution in their demand function, since there is no clean substitute on the market. Overall, it seems reasonable to assume that competition and free entry increase the chances of the clean technology being present on the market, and thus decreasing $D_c(P)$. Indeed, if there is free entry, there is room for ecological certification and green labeling; a firm may choose to enter the market and to produce the good with the clean technology. It may be a government responsibility to make room for efficient competition practices. Note, however, that a fully clean substitute may not exist. In this case, there is a risk of a rebound effect: the consumption of the "clean" good increases more than the decrease of the polluting good, which may increase pollution overall.

Second, in order to sanction an increase in the influence of political consumerism, facilitating the emergence of credible and trustworthy ecological certification may be an effective policy. Governments may choose to create directly certified labels, or ensure the quality of labels by creating control organizations and designing comprehensive and clear sets of rules defining labeled products. As Schumacher (2010) concludes: "It might be useful to raise the general awareness of ecolabeling and standardize it for easy comparison. ... this would help in generating a substantially larger amount of public awareness than is currently the case." For example, the European Union defines the process by which agricultural products may be labeled as organic. In order to have the right to use the organic logo of the European Union, the producer has to pass a strict certification process. Every farmer has to be inspected by a public or private authority that has been approved by the member state. Overall, the European Union designs and monitors the whole certification process, and publicizes it, with the objective of informing consumers about the trustworthiness of organic food (European Commission 2008). Public policies may help here to reduce transaction costs related to political consumerism, and thus increase its efficiency, making a case of good complementarity.

Finally, it is interesting to note that environmental policies sometimes create unexpected coalitions between green consumers and corporate industry. This is the case when public policies tend not only to improve the state of the environment, but also to benefit some key actors in the market. For instance, some firms may lobby for the implementation of environmental policies, as a strategy to increase their rivals' costs (Salop and Scheffman 1983). This kind of situation was observed in the late 1980s, when US firms in the tuna industry lobbied for a more stringent environmental legislation to protect dolphins, with a view to increasing the costs of smaller domestic competitors and to securing an embargo on Mexican imports (Korber 1998). In a comparable manner, labels and certificates have been used in the past as non-tariff trade barriers, such as the Flower Label Program in Germany (Gandhi 2006).

5.5   Conclusion

Political consumerism may take several forms, from green consumption to consumer boycotts, and represents a way to integrate consumers' environmental and social preferences into markets. Political consumerism refers to voluntary approaches to environmental issues, as compared to mandatory approaches such as taxes. Even if these consumption patterns are assuming an ever growing importance and have a non-negligible impact on market outcomes, they nevertheless do not seem to constitute an efficient substitute for public policies. Indeed, individual behaviors are difficult to coordinate, and people concerned by political consumerism are certainly of insufficient importance to represent every citizen efficiently and fairly.

However, political consumerism may be a key complement to public policies. First, governments may create the conditions to maximize political consumerism efficiency, by helping the emergence of trustworthy certification and facilitating information and education; that is, by influencing the perception of what constitutes the agent's self interest (Etzioni 1988) and by establishing routinized behaviors, providing information to agents, thus reducing uncertainty (Tacconi 1997). Second, they may reduce the cost of political consumerism by implementing relevant fiscal policies to make polluting consumption more costly and green consumption cheaper. Overall, political consumerism has a potentially important role to play in mitigating environmental degradation, which should be taken into account in the implementation of public policies. European environmental policy already implicitly integrates this potential complementarity, mixing soft and traditional environmental policies, and favoring market-based environmental management and structuring markets.

In the light of this chapter, it can thus be argued that political consumerism is more likely to be efficient in markets where consumers' preferences are close to social preferences, where market structure is more competitive – to increase market diversity and facilitate the emergence of trustworthy certification, and where information is more transparent – for instance in the case of search or experience attributes rather than credence ones. Moreover, political consumerism may be considered as targeted contraction: sectors related to environmental and social harm tend to contract, while sectors implying little or no negative externalities may continue to grow.

This chapter clears the way for further research about the complementarity of public policies and political consumerism. Do markets with higher levels of environmental taxes also experience higher levels of political consumerism? To what extent does environmental taxation facilitate the switch from polluting consumption to greener consumption? Do markets experiencing higher political consumption – through certified goods, for instance – also experience lower prices of tradable permits? Being one of the rare consumers with market power, are states and public sectors able to impact markets through political consumerism, as when they choose to forbid imports of non-certified timber?

References

Ariely, D. and Norton, M. I. (2009) Conceptual consumption. *Annual Review of Psychology*, 60: 475–99.

Baek, Y. M. (2010) To buy or not to buy: Who are political consumers? What do they think and how do they participate? *Political Studies*, 58: 1065–86.

Baldwin, R. (2008) Regulation lite: The rise of emissions trading. *Law and Financial Markets Review*, 2(3).

Begaudin, S. and Demontrand, P. R. (2007) Le concept de référentiels sociétaux: Principes et enjeux de leur intégration en tant que critère d'achat par la grande distribution. *Revue Française de Marketing*, 212.5.

Bishop, M. (2004) *Essential Economics*. London: Profile Books.

Börkey, P., Glachant, M. and Lévêque, F. (2000) Voluntary approaches for environmental policy in OECD countries: An assessment. Centre d'Economie Industrielle, Ecole Nationale Supérieure des Mines de Paris.

Bougherara, D., Costa, S., Grolleau, G. and Ibanez, L. (2009) Dealing with aversion to the sucker's payoff in public goods games. *Economics Bulletin*, 29(4): 3194–3202.

Braathen, N. A. (2005) Environmental agreements used in combination with other policy instruments. In *The Handbook of Environmental Voluntary Agreements: Design, Implementation and Evaluation Issues*, Environment and Policy Series, Volume 43. Dordrecht: Springer Netherlands.

Brennan, T. J. (2006) "Green" preferences as regulatory policy instrument. *Ecological Economics*, 56: 144–54.

Buenstorf, G. and Cordes, C. (2008) Can sustainable consumption be learned? A model of cultural evolution. *Ecological Economics*, 67: 646–57.

Charles, E. (2009) Eco-labelling: A new deal for a more durable fishery management? *Ocean and Coastal Management*, 52(5): 250–7.

Chiroleu-Assouline M. (2007) Efficacité Comparée des Instruments de Régulation Environnementale. Note de Synthèse du SESP no. 167.

Coad, A., de Haan, P. and Woersdorfer, J. S. (2009) Consumer support for environmental policies: An application to purchases of green cars. *Ecological Economics*, 68: 2078–86.

Conrad, K. (2001) Voluntary Environmental agreements vs. emission taxes in strategic trade models. *Environmental and Resources Economics*, 19: 361–81.

Cogoy, M. (1999) The consumer as a social and environmental actor. *Ecological Economics*, 28: 385–398.

Downs, A. (1957) *An Economic Theory of Democracy*. New York: Harper & Row.

European Commission (2007) *Green Paper on Market-Based Instruments for Environment and Related Policy Purposes*. http://eur-lex.europa.eu/LexUriServ/LexUriServ.do?uri=COM:2007:0140:FIN:EN:PDF

European Commission (2008) *A Guide for Stakeholders, Farmers, Processors and Distributors*. http://ec.europa.eu/agriculture/organic/

Etzioni, A. (1988) *The Moral Dimension: Toward a New Economics*. New York: Free Press.

Ferrando y Puig, J. and Giamporcaro-Saunière, S. (2005) *Pour une "Autre" Consommation: Sens et Emergence d'une Consommation Politique*. Paris: L'Harmattan.

Fitoussi, J. P., Laurent, E. and Le Cacheux, J. (2007) La Stratégie Environnementale de l'Union Européenne. Document de travail OFCE no. 2007–04. Observatoire Français des Conjonctures Economiques, Paris.

Friedman, M. (1996) Positive approach to organized consumer action: The "buycott" as an alternative to the boycott. *Journal of Consumer Policy*, 19(4): 439–51.

Gandhi, S. R. (2006) Disciplining voluntary environmental standards at the WTO: an Indian legal viewpoint. Working Paper 181, Indian Council for Research on International Economic Relations.

Grolleau, G., Mzoughi, N. and Thiébaut, L. (2004) Les instruments volontaires: un nouveau mode de régulation de l'environnement. *Revue Internationale de Droit Economique*, pp. 461–481.

Holzer, B. (2006) Political consumerism between individual choice and collective action: Social movements, role mobilisation and signalling. *International Journal of Consumer Studies*, 405–415.

Howley, P., Hynes, S. and O Donoghue, C. (2010) The citizen versus consumer distinction: An exploration of individuals' preferences in contingent valuation studies. *Ecological Economics*, 69(7): 1524–31.

Innes, R. (2006) A theory of consumer boycotts under symmetric information and imperfect competition. *Economic Journal*, 116: 355–81.

Jensen, H. R. (2005) What does political consumerism mean for marketers. IEBC 2005: 4th Annual International Business and Economy Conference, Honolulu, Hawaii, USA.

Johannsen, K. S. (2002) Combining Voluntary agreements and taxes – an evaluation of the Danish agreement scheme on energy efficiency in industry. *Journal of Cleaner Production*, 10(2).

Johansson, B. (2000) *Economic Instruments in Practice 1: Carbon Tax in Sweden*, Swedish Environmental Protection Agency.

Korber, A. (1998) Why everyone loves Flipper. *European Journal of Political Economy*, 14(3): 475–509.

Lee, W. L. and Yik, F. W. H. (2004) Regulatory and voluntary approaches for enhancing building energy efficiency. *Progress in Energy and Combustion Science*, 30: 477–99.

Linott, J. (1998) Beyond the economics of more: The place of consumption in ecological economics. *Ecological Economics*, 25: 239–48.

Micheletti, M. (2002) Consumer choice as political participation. Seminarium: Medborgardeltagande i den Representativa Demokratin. *Statsvetenskaplig Tidskrift*, 105(3): 218–34.

Micheletti, M. (2003) *Political Virtue and Shopping. Individuals, Consumerism and Collective Action*. New York: Palgrave Macmillan.

Micheletti, M. and Stolle, D. (2008) Fashioning social justice through political consumerism, capitalism, and the internet. *Cultural Studies*, 22: 5–6.

Micheletti, M., Follesdal, A. and Stolle, D. (eds) (2004) *Politics, Products and Markets: Exploring the Political Consumerism Past and Present*. New Brunswick, NJ: Transaction Publishers.

Mylondo, B. (2005) *Des Caddies et des Hommes: Consommation Citoyenne Contre Société de Consommation*. Paris: La Dispute.

Nielson, L. A. (2010) Boycott or buycott? Understanding political consumerism. *Journal of Consumer Behavior*, 9: 214–27.

OECD (2003) *Voluntary Approaches for Environmental Policy: Effectiveness, Efficiency and Usage in Policy Mixes*. Paris: Organisation for Economic Co-operation and Development.

Pachauri, R. (2008) Comment les Pays Pauvres Vont-ils Affronter le Défi Climatique? *Télérama*, 3027.11, 17 January. http://www.telerama.fr/monde/24348comment_les_pays_pauvres_vont_ils_affronter_le_defi_climatique.php?xtor=RSS-26

Pigou, A. C. (1920/2002) *The Economics of Welfare*. New Brunswick, NJ: Transaction.

Riera, P., Aranda, L. and Mavsar, R. (2007) Efficiency and equity of forest policies: A graphic analysis using the partial equilibrium framework. *Forest Policy and Economics*, 9: 852–61.

Rose, N. (1999) *Powers of Freedom*. New York: Cambridge University Press.

Sagoff, M. (1988) *The Economy of the Earth: Philosophy, Law, and the Environment*. New York: Cambridge Community Press.

Salop S. C. and Scheffman, D. T. (1983) Raising rivals' costs, *American Economic Review Papers and Proceedings*, 73: 267–71.

Schumacher, I. (2010) Ecolabeling, consumers' preferences and taxation. *Ecological Economics*, 69: 2202–12.

Spangenberg, J. H. and Lorek, S. (2002) Environmentally sustainable households consumption: From aggregate environmental pressures to priority fields of action. *Ecological Economics*, 43: 127–40.

Strømsnes, K. (2009) Political consumerism: A substitute for or supplement to conventional political participation. *Journal of Civil Society*, 5(3): 303–14.

Tacconi, L. (1997) An ecological economic approach to forest and biodiverstity conservation: The case of Vanuatu. *World Development*, 25(12): 1995–2008.

Theron, J. M. (2010) Political consumerism: Possibilities for international norm change. Master's Degree in Political Science Thesis, University of Stellenbosch, South Africa.

Turner, T. (1995) Neoliberal ecopolitics and indigenous people: The Kayapo, the rainforest harvest and the Bodyshop. *Yale F&ES Bulletin*, 98: 113–27.

Welsch, H. and Kühling, J. (2009) Determinants of pro-environmental consumption: The role of reference groups and routine behaviours. *Ecological Economics*, 69: 166–76.

Wu, J. (1999) The relative efficiency of voluntary vs mandatory environmental regulations. *Journal of Environmental Economics and Management*, 38: 158–75.

6 On the sources of consumer boycotts ineffectiveness

This chapter was published in *Journal of Environment and Development*, 18(3) (2009).

6.1 Introduction

A *consumer boycott* (Friedman 1991, 1999), i.e. the individual or collective choice not to buy some product, is a tool frequently used by non-governmental organizations (NGOs), lobby groups or individual citizens to protest against perceived unfair marketing, social or environmental practices. Cosmetics firms are boycotted for their use of animal testing (Davidson, 1995); major oil companies have been targeted for their environmental damage and their supposed lobbying efforts to deter climate change policies (Skjærseth and Skodvin 2001); some large fast-food companies have been boycotted because of their supposed environmentally unfriendly meat production methods (Garrett 1987); and NGOs support the boycott of non-certified tropical timber to protest against unsustainable harvest practices and corruption (Klooster 2005).

The literature on consumer boycotts mainly focuses on field studies (Pruitt and Friedman 1986; Garrett 1987; Koku *et al.* 1997; Teoh *et al.* 1999) or history (Friedman 1985, 1995; Smith 1990). Tyran and Engelmann (2005) provide an experimental analysis.

Theoretical investigations of consumer boycotts remain rare. Innes (2006) considers a duopoly setting where firms choose between a clean and a dirty technology, while environmental organizations may invest in consumer boycotts to deter the choice of the dirty technology. The effectiveness of the boycott is determined mainly by the environmental organization's investment. Baron (2002) considers that the action of boycotting by some consumers provides information to other citizens about the seriousness of a situation. Boycotting allows consumers to signal their private information.

More serious issues thus enhance stronger and longer boycotts. Diermeier and Van Mieghem (2005) describe coordination among boycotting consumers as a stochastic process with threshold effects.

By analyzing the conditions under which a consumer boycott is effective, this chapter points out the main sources of the ineffectiveness of consumer boycotts. We consider a boycott effective if it induces a change in the targeted firm's behavior consistent with the boycotting group's objectives. Therefore, we focus on market-oriented boycotts and do not discuss media-oriented boycotts, the aim of which is only to signal disapproval and to increase public awareness. By way of illustration, we focus on environmental motivations, but consumer boycotts based on social and health considerations follow the same analysis.

Two main conclusions can be given. First, as with any other type of collective action, free riding and coordination failures are major problems of consumer boycotts. Second, even if these problems can be avoided, a simple tradeoff between the opportunity cost of boycotting and the boycott's potential to hurt the firm's profit reduces considerably the boycott's potential for success. Thus, consumers able to hurt the targeted firm's profit are unlikely to participate, while some consumers with low cost of boycotting do participate, but have a fairly small potential to make it succeed.

Section 6.2 underlines the fact that free riding and coordination issues are major problems of consumer boycotts. Section 6.3 presents consumer boycotts as a complete information war of attrition model. Finally, the analysis is applied to real-life boycotts in Section 6.4. Section 6.5 concludes.

6.2   Boycotts and collective action shortcomings

The potential success of consumer boycotts is crucially limited by the usual issues of collective action. Indeed, choosing to boycott is an individual and costly decision, while the success of the boycott is determined by collective action. This dichotomy naturally implies a temptation to free-ride and a risk of coordination failure. We are here in the framework of critical mass models (see Granovetter 1978).

Consider a firm producing a good with a polluting technology, while a clean technology is available. An environmental NGO announces a consumer boycott, whereby any consumer not satisfied with the use of the dirty technology stops consuming the good. The existence of an imperfect substitute is assumed. Thus, only one firm is boycotted (or perhaps a set of homogeneous firms), and market competition is implicitly considered trough the quality of the available substitute.

There are N environmentalists who would prefer the firm to switch to the clean technology. Environmentalist consumers are heterogeneous in their boycotting costs and gains from a successful boycott.[1] Boycotting consists of paying a cost (C_i) for sure (i.e. not consuming the good) to receive a potential gain G_i (i.e. the technology switch in the event of success). An individual environmentalist participates if the expected payoff of participating exceeds the expected payoff of not participating.

Consumer i's individual choice is to boycott ($B_i = 1$) or not boycott ($B_i = 0$). The number of boycotting consumers is therefore

$$n = \sum_{i=1}^{N} B_i \tag{6.1}$$

The firm will switch technology if the boycott is sufficiently important, i.e. if the boycotting population is greater than or equal to n^s. This threshold at which the boycott is successful is unknown to the environmentalists. However, the boycott's probability of success depends on the size of the boycotting population: $p[n \geq n^s]$. The probability of success is zero if nobody boycotts: $p[0 \geq n^s] = 0$. The boycott would be successful for sure if every environmentalist participated in the boycott: $p[N \geq n^s] = 1$.[2] Moreover, the current number of boycotting consumers n is public knowledge. Thus, the boycott is potentially successful.

However, as we will see in the rest of this section, free riding and the lack of coordination may jeopardize the success potential of the boycott.

6.2.1 Boycott and free riding

In a similar manner to the voter's paradox mechanism, free riding is a major cause of boycott failures. Any individual consumer considers two potential choices and four related outcomes. First, the consumer can ignore the boycott and continue to consume the good. Second, he can decide to boycott. In either case, the boycott could succeed or fail. Boycotting is costly in terms of utility, since the consumer has to switch his consumption for an imperfect substitute, providing less utility. Moreover, the success of the boycott is highly uncertain, and individual participation of any consumer only has a marginal impact on the probability of success. In other words, any individual has an incentive to free-ride, i.e. not to participate in the boycott while hoping for it to succeed.

Indeed, any environmentalist i boycotts ($B_i = 1$) if

$$p\left[\sum_{i \neq -i} B_{-i} + 1 \geq n^s\right] G_i - C_i \geq p\left[\sum_{i \neq -i} B_{-i} \geq n^s\right] G_i \tag{6.2}$$

The participation threshold $\overline{p}_i = \frac{C_i}{G_i}$ at which consumer i decides to boycott is

$$p\left[\sum_{i \neq -i} B_{-i} + 1 \geq n^s\right] - p\left[\sum_{i \neq -i} B_{-i} \geq n^s\right] \geq \overline{p}_i \qquad (6.3)$$

The choice of any individual consumer only increases marginally the probability of a boycott success. Thus, the left-hand side of equation (6.3) is close to zero, and only consumers with very small or negative threshold $\overline{p}_i$ participate in the boycott. As a consequence, only consumers with very strong environmental preferences are expected to boycott, and the success of the boycott is highly improbable.

Solving free-riding issues is a crucial and complex concern in this case. Indeed, consumption behaviors are not observable and social control is thus impossible. NGO communication may help reduce this concern, if trying to emphasize individual responsibility in the boycott. However, even if free riding is avoided, consumers still need to coordinate.

6.2.2   Coordination failure

A second crucial issue concerning boycott successes is the lack of coordination. Indeed, individual consumers being disseminated, direct coordination is not possible. In contrast to the previous subsection, individual consumers only consider the gain from a boycott success if they participate. Thus, we avoid the voter's paradox and free riding that have been considered before.

Consumer i decides to boycott at time t ($B_i(t) = 1$) if his potential gain from a successful boycott exceeds his cost of boycotting. The number of boycotting consumers at time t is $n(t) = \sum_{i=1}^{N} B_i(t)$. The individual choice of boycotting still depends on the probability of the boycott being successful. The participation threshold $\overline{p}_i = \frac{C_i}{G_i}$ at which consumer i decides to boycott is here:

$$\begin{cases} B_i(t) = 1 \text{ if } p[n(t) \geq n^s] \geq \overline{p}_i \\ B_i(t) = 0 \text{ if } p[n(t) \geq n^s] < \overline{p}_i \end{cases} \qquad (6.4)$$

Consumers will thus enter sequentially in the boycott. Strong environmentalists, who have low costs of boycotting and small participation thresholds, will participate first. As the importance of the boycott and the probability of success grow, consumers with higher thresholds decide to participate. Therefore, the last consumer $\overline{n}$ deciding to boycott is defined as follows:

$$\bar{n} : p[\bar{n} \geq n^s] = \bar{p}_n \qquad (6.5)$$

$\bar{n}$ also defines the equilibrium boycott participation, which is the population with participation threshold larger than the expected probability of success. Figure 6.1 gives a representation of the equilibrium boycott population, which is the intersection between $p[n(t) \geq n^s]$ and $\bar{p}_i$. The boycott is successful if $\bar{n} \geq n^s$. Overall, this equilibrium boycott participation and thus the potential for success depend on the distribution of boycotting costs and the structure of beliefs. Optimistic beliefs about the firm's withdrawal threshold n^s may compensate for the lack of coordination. Moreover, the distribution of consumers needs to have fat tails, i.e. a large number of strong environmentalists, with low participation thresholds.

Figure 6.2 gives an example of coordination failure leading to an unsuccessful boycott. The boycott would be successful if every environmentalist participated. However, the distribution of consumers (uniform in the case of Figure 6.2) and the structure of beliefs (normal distribution) are such that

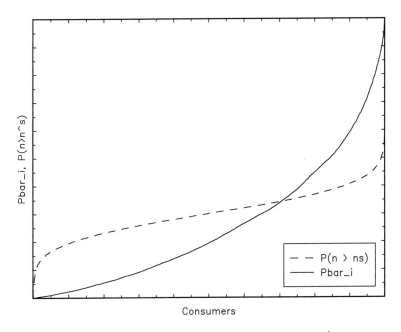

Figure 6.1 Equilibrium boycott population, *Parameters: $\bar{p}$: Chi^2 distribution, $p[n(t) \geq n^s]$: normal distribution, $N = 10,000, \bar{n} = 7,296$.*

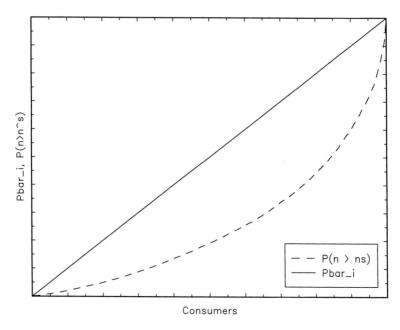

Figure 6.2 Unsuccessful boycott due to coordination failure, *Parameters:* $\overline{p}$: *uniform distribution,* $p[n(t) \geq n^s]$: *normal distribution,* $N = 10{,}000, \overline{n} = 0.$

nobody decides to boycott in equilibrium (because $p[n(t) \geq n^s] < \overline{p}_i, \forall i \in [0, N]$).

Overall, one can easily see that a potentially successful boycott may be ineffective due to the lack of coordination, even if a boycott success is also a potential equilibrium. Coordination failures are also difficult to compensate for. Communication efforts to enhance optimistic beliefs and information raising environmental preferences may help to solve those issues. However, even if free-riding problems and coordination failures are solved, boycotts are not likely to succeed.

6.3   Boycott as a war of attrition with perfect information

We now focus on a best-case scenario, with no free riding or lack of coordination. Moreover, information is now assumed to be perfect. Thus, gains and costs of both players are common knowledge. In this context, consumer boycotts can be considered as a war of attrition between a group of consumers and the firm targeted.[3] However, this model differs from usual war of attrition models, in the sense that we consider asymmetric motivations and payoffs (Burton 2004).

A war of attrition is a model of aggression between two players. The game takes the form of a succession of identical periods. The model is stationary: each period represents the same type of problem for both players, with no information gain or change in costs or benefits. Both players make conjectures about their opponent's strategy.

6.3.1 *Technology choice and consumer behavior*

FIRM'S TECHNOLOGY CHOICE

Technology 1 (T1) is cheap but polluting, while technology 2 (T2) is clean but more expensive. A firm chooses technology 1 if it generates larger profit than technology 2, i.e. $\pi_1 > \pi_2$. The profit schedules, π_1 and π_2, differ simply because the production costs, the price of the good and the demand structure are not the same whether the good is produced with the dirty or the clean technology.[4]

CONSUMPTION PATTERNS

The consumer population is of size 1, with two homogeneous groups. The environmentalists represent an exogenous share α of the population. The environmentalists' utility is increasing in consumption and decreasing in pollution. Moreover, they would prefer the firm to produce with technology 2: $U_1 < U_2$, where U_1 is the utility derived by an environmentalist if the good is produced with T1, and U_2 is the utility for a good produced with T2.

A proportion $1 - \alpha$ of consumers only considers individual consumption in its utility function. Therefore, these consumers prefer the firm to use T1, because they do not care about pollution and T1 is cheaper. Thus, they would never participate in an eventual boycott. Appendix 6A presents basic consumer theory illustrating links between environmental preferences and consumption.

BOYCOTT AS A WAR OF ATTRITION

An environmental organization announces a consumer boycott, whereby any consumer unsatisfied with the use of technology 1 stops consuming the good. Boycotting consumers switch their consumption of the good to the consumption of an imperfect substitute produced with a clean technology but providing lower utility. The utility of a boycotting consumer is U_b. The cost of boycotting is thus the difference between the utility derived by the consumption of the good and the utility of boycotting: $\Delta U = U_1 - U_b$.

This specification of an exogenous substitute allows a wide variety of market structures to be considered. At one extreme, the targeted firm is in a monopoly position, and there is no substitute available on the market, which means a high boycotting cost. At the other extreme, if the market is very competitive and differentiated, there is room for ecological certification: a firm may provide the good considered with a clean production, which involves no boycotting cost. More generally, a better substitute provides higher utility of boycotting.

Moreover, the action of boycotting may have a utility in itself, consisting of social or psychological satisfaction generated by political activity. Transaction costs may also increase the cost of boycotting. For example, multiple certification is likely to decrease the utility of boycotting, as it may be time-consuming for the consumer to find which is the best substitute on the market.

$\lambda \gamma \pi_1$ is the residual profit of the firm under boycott. γ is the residual profit share when every environmentalist participates in the boycott ($\gamma \leq 1$) and λ is an exogenous efficiency parameter measuring the environmental organization's capacity to coordinate consumers: $1 \leq \lambda \leq \frac{1}{\gamma}$. The environmental organization is totally efficient in coordinating consumers if $\lambda = 1$, while there is full coordination failure if $\lambda = \frac{1}{\gamma}$. The direct cost of being boycotted is therefore the difference between the profit when producing with T1 and the profit when being boycotted: $\Delta \pi_1 = (1 - \lambda \gamma)\pi_1$.

A crucial element in determining one player's conjecture is the other player's maximum conflict duration, which is the point in time after which this player would never plan to stay in the game. Indeed, net cumulative payoffs being decreasing with time, there is a point in time at which these payoffs become negative. T^f is the firm's maximum conflict duration and T^c is the consumers' maximum boycott duration.

6.3.2   *Maximum conflict durations*

The firm's net cumulative payoff of winning the conflict after T periods, $B^f(T)$, consists of the smaller profit received during the boycott for T periods and the larger profit of keeping T1 forever, minus the payoff of the alternative strategy, which is the cumulative discounted profit of switching immediately to T2:

$$B^f(T) = \sum_{t=0}^{T-1} \rho^t \lambda \gamma \pi_1 + \sum_{t=T}^{\infty} \rho^t \pi_1 - \sum_{t=0}^{\infty} \rho^t \pi_2 \qquad (6.6)$$

where ρ is the discounting factor. The maximum conflict duration of the firm is the point in time at which its cumulative net payoff becomes negative:

$$T^f = \frac{1}{\ln \rho} \ln \left(\frac{\pi_2 - \lambda \gamma \pi_1}{(1 - \lambda \gamma) \pi_1} \right) \tag{6.7}$$

The environmentalists' net payoff of winning the game after T periods consists of the discounted utility of boycotting for T periods, plus the cumulative utility of having the good produced with T2 forever, net of the alternative strategy's payoff, which is the discounted cumulative utility of never boycotting:

$$B^c(T) = \sum_{t=0}^{T-1} \rho^t U_b + \sum_{t=T}^{\infty} \rho^t U_2 - \sum_{t=0}^{\infty} \rho^t U_1 \tag{6.8}$$

The maximum boycott duration is thus

$$T^c = \frac{1}{\ln \rho} \ln \left(\frac{U_1 - U_b}{U_2 - U_b} \right) \tag{6.9}$$

6.3.3 Game equilibrium

We first determine responses to each player's conjectures, and then which strategy both players actually choose.

RESPONSE TO CONJECTURES

Suppose that the firm believes that the consumers' chosen strategy is to boycott for a strictly positive duration $\hat{D}^c$, and then to withdraw. The firm has to decide to remain in the conflict for $\hat{D}^c + 1$ periods, or to withdraw immediately. Indeed, withdrawing immediately is preferable to remaining fewer than $\hat{D}^c$ periods. If the maximum duration of the firm is less than or equal to the conjecture on the consumer boycott length, $T^f < \hat{D}^c$, the best strategy for the firm is to withdraw immediately.

Similarly, consumers may conjecture that the firm has chosen to remain in the conflict for $\hat{D}^f$ periods, and then withdraw. If the maximum boycott duration is shorter than this conjecture, $T^c < \hat{D}^f$, the best strategy for the consumers is not to boycott at all.

STRATEGY CHOICE

To succeed, both players have to choose a longer duration than their conjecture: $D^f > \hat{D}^c$, $D^c \geq \hat{D}^f$. This is known to both players, who also know the maximum durations T^f and T^c.

"A rational player will use those strategies that are best responses to some beliefs he might have about the strategies of his opponents" (Fudenberg and Tirole 1991). Therefore, it is not rationalizable for both players to conjecture a duration that is shorter than the shortest maximum duration $(\min(T^c, T^f))$.

Thus, if the firm has the shortest maximum duration $T^f < T^c$, both players can conclude that consumers will choose a longer duration, $\hat{D}^c > T^f$. In this case, the firm would be better off withdrawing immediately, resulting in a successful boycott.

If the maximum boycott duration of the consumers is shorter than the maximum conflict duration of the firm $T^c < T^f$, the boycott cannot be successful, since the best response for an environmentalist is never to boycott, while the firm's best response is always to keep T1. Conversely, for a maximum boycott duration longer than the firm's maximum duration, the best response for the consumers is always to boycott, while the firm's best response is to switch immediately to T2. The boycott is therefore successful if $T^f \leq T^c$. In order to avoid mixed strategies and to focus on pure strategies, we assume that the firm has an implicit preference for compromise: for $T^c = T^f$, the firm would be the one to withdraw.

The outcome of the game is therefore determined at the first period, which is somehow disappointing for the description of real-life boycotts. Nevertheless, this setup describes the necessary conditions of the demand patterns for a successful boycott.

6.3.4   *Outcome of the game*

Depending on utilities and profits, several outcomes may be considered (see Table 6.1). First, if $\pi_2 > \pi_1$, technology 2 is more profitable than technology 1, and the boycott makes no sense (row 1). Second, if $U_1 > U_2$, T1 is preferred by the consumers, therefore there is no boycott and the firm keeps using T1 (row 2).

Third, for $\pi_2 \leq \lambda\gamma\pi_1$, the boycott is not costly enough (or coordination is too weak) for the firm to introduce the technology change. Indeed, if the decrease in the firm's profit is too small, the firm always chooses to keep the polluting technology whatever the behavior of the environmentalists (rows 3 and 4). Fourth, if $U_b > U_1$, the environmentalists always boycott, whatever the firm's strategy. In that case, the boycotting cost is negative,

Table 6.1 The consumers' utility and the firm's profit determine the game outcome

Utility $\Rightarrow T^c$	Profit $\Rightarrow T^f$	Outcome
	$\pi_2 > \pi_1 \Rightarrow T^f < 0$	T2 chosen by the firm
$U_1 > U_2 \Rightarrow T^c < 0$		T1 preferred by the consumers
$U_1 > U_b \Rightarrow T^c > 0$	$\pi_2 \leq \lambda \gamma \pi_1 \Rightarrow T^f \to \infty$	T1 always kept, no boycott
$U_1 < U_b \Rightarrow T^c \to \infty$	$\pi_2 \leq \lambda \gamma \pi_1 \Rightarrow T^f \to \infty$	T1 always kept, always boycott
$U_1 < U_b \Rightarrow T^c \to \infty$	$\pi_2 > \lambda \gamma \pi_1 \Rightarrow T^f > 0$	Boycott successful
$U_1 > U_b \Rightarrow T^c > 0$	$\pi_2 > \lambda \gamma \pi_1 \Rightarrow T^f > 0$	Boycott successful if $T^c \geq T^f$
		Boycott ineffective if $T^c < T^f$

meaning that consumers derive positive net utility from boycotting (rows 4 and 5).

Otherwise (row 6), i.e. for $U_1 > U_b$ and $\lambda \gamma \pi_1 < \pi_2$, the outcome of the game is determined by factors influencing the two maximum lengths T^f (see Appendix 6B) and T^c (Appendix 6C). When considering the firm's maximum duration, a more profitable clean technology decreases T^f: $\frac{\partial T^f}{\partial \pi_2} < 0$. Conversely, a more profitable dirty technology increases T^f: $\frac{\partial T^f}{\partial \pi_1} > 0$. Finally, T^f is larger if the residual profit under boycott is large and the environmental organization inefficient to coordinate consumers: $\frac{\partial T^f}{\partial \gamma} > 0, \frac{\partial T^f}{\partial \lambda} > 0$. When focusing on the consumers' maximum boycott duration, a larger utility derived from the clean technology increases T^c: $\frac{\partial T^c}{\partial U_2} > 0$. Moreover, a smaller T1 utility also increases T^c: $\frac{\partial T^c}{\partial U_1} < 0$. Finally, a higher utility of boycotting increases T^c, by decreasing the boycott opportunity cost: $\frac{\partial T^c}{\partial U_b} > 0$.

6.3.5 What makes a boycott successful?

This subsection analyzes which factors influence major determinants of the maximum durations T^c and T^f. Factors increasing T^c raise the boycott's likelihood of success, while factors increasing T^f decrease this likelihood.

QUALITY OF THE SUBSTITUTE

The quality of the substitute directly decreases the cost of boycotting (increases T^c). Thus, it unambiguously increases the potential for success. Our specification does not consider the market structure explicitly. However, considering an imperfect substitute allows for flexibility in the analysis. At one extreme, if the firm is in a monopoly position, there is no substitute and $U_b = 0$ (assuming boycotting provides no utility by itself). At the other extreme, if the firm plays in a very differentiated market, there is room for ecological certification or labeling, and another firm may enter and provide the good with a clean production. The exploitation of this niche would imply $U_b \geq U_2 > U_1$. Then the environmentalists would always choose to boycott, because the boycott would be costless. Therefore, boycotts are more likely to succeed if the targeted firm plays in a very differentiated and competitive market than if the firm is a monopoly.

SELF-IMAGE

Boycotting may have a utility *per se*. Indeed, collective action participation to improve the quality of the environment is likely to improve the environmentalists' self-image, which is positively correlated with U_b.

TRANSACTION COSTS

Potentially important transaction costs may reduce the utility of boycotting. The substitute, even if of good quality, may be quite difficult to find on the market. Moreover, if several different substitutes are available on the market, in the case of multiple certification, it may be time-consuming to find the best substitute available.

PROPORTION OF ENVIRONMENTALISTS IN THE POPULATION

A large number of environmentalists (α) unambiguously raises the boycott's potential for success. Indeed, a large boycotting population unambiguously decreases the residual profit (increases γ). Therefore, it decreases the maximum duration of the firm (T^f).

ENVIRONMENTAL PREFERENCES AND LEVELS OF CONSUMPTION

Environmental preferences have an ambiguous effect on the boycott's success potential. As mentioned in Appendix 6A, stronger environmental preferences imply a lower level of polluting consumption. It follows naturally that the environmentalists have lower costs of boycotting (larger T^c) if they have stronger environmental preferences, simply because they have smaller amounts of consumption to renounce, but enjoy the involved pollution reduction more. Thus, consumers with strong environmental preferences are more likely to boycott than others.

However, because they have lower levels of consumption, their action of boycotting will have a smaller impact on the firm's profit (larger γ). Thus, stronger environmental preferences tend to increase the firm's maximum duration (T^f): the targeted firm does not care about being boycotted by consumers with low levels of consumption.

Overall, consumers with stronger environmental preferences tend to participate more readily in consumer boycotts, but their impact on the firm's profit is smaller. In the light of this proposition, it is easier to understand the existence of infinite consumer boycotts that never succeed. Take the example of the boycott of major oil companies because of their lobbying against climate change policies. The consumers most likely to boycott these companies are those who feel the highest negative utility from pollution. Even if no boycott is announced, these consumers are likely to prefer using their bicycles or public transport to the frequent use of their car, and their capacity to hurt the companies' profit is small. Conversely, consumers with the highest ability to hurt the firms profit consume a lot of oil, and thus have high opportunity cost, which makes their participation in the boycott unlikely.

6.4   Case studies

In the light of the previous insights, in this section we consider past boycott experiences.

6.4.1   *Shell and the Brent Spar case*

In 1995, Shell Oil was planning to sink a 14,500 ton oil platform in the North Atlantic sea. The environmental organization Greanpeace initiated a vast protest movement to oppose this plan. Activists occupied the Brent Spar platform, 200 Shell service stations were threatened in Germany, and a widespread boycott of Shell took place. After a few months, Shell canceled its plan for deep sea disposal and decided to recycle the entire structure (Zyglidopoulos 2002).

Several insights in this chapter can help explain this boycott success. First, oil is quite a homogeneous good, and service stations are easy to find almost anywhere. Therefore, one can consider that the non-polluting substitute (i.e. oil companies not sinking the platform) is perfect, and the only transaction cost is going from any Shell station to the next service station. Overall, boycotting Shell was costless ($U_b \geq U_1$).

Moreover, sinking costs (π_1) were estimated at £18 million, while the alternative method costs (π_2) were estimated at £69 million (Zyglidopoulos 2002). Considering the fact that Shell is a worldwide multinational, perhaps this difference in costs was quite small compared to the size and importance of the boycotting population (small γ).

In other words, Shell was almost costless to boycott and easy to hurt, which may explain why the Brent Spar case is often considered as an example of a successful boycott.

6.4.2   Cosmetic firms and animal testing

Animal testing is common practice in several industries, such as cosmetics and pharmaceuticals (Davidson 1995).

Following the analysis in this chapter, this type of consumer boycott has very little chance of success. Indeed, boycotting firms using animal testing is almost equivalent to boycotting the entire cosmetics sector. Good substitutes (cosmetics from firms not using animal testing) are therefore difficult to find and transaction costs are likely to be high. For example, Ahimsa, a French organization lobbying for animal protection, lists more than 200 firms testing their products on animals (cosmetics firms and others). Note first that it is difficult to perfectly memorize a 200-firm list. There is therefore a problem of clarity of the boycott, which creates important transaction costs, as it seems difficult to go shopping using a list of 200 boycotted firms (decreasing T^c). Moreover, alternative strategies to animal testing, although an important research topic (see Johns Hopkins Center for Alternatives to Animal Testing), may still be very costly (increasing T^f).

Overall, boycotting firms using animal testing should not be very effective, especially because of high transaction costs, due to a lack of clarity in the boycott and difficulties of purchase $=$ ing good substitutes. It is thus likely that only strong environmentalists will participate in this type of boycott and that their ability to hurt will be quite small.

6.4.3   Boycott of non-certified timber

Several NGOs militate for a boycott of non-certified tropical timber (Klooster 2005). Indeed, illegal logging in developing countries plagues local development and degrades forest resources. This type of boycott at first appears to be a perfect case for a success. Indeed, timber is quite a homogeneous good. Moreover, ecological timber certification offers good substitutes. Overall, the cost of boycotting non-certified tropical timber seems to be quite low (related to large T^c).

However, a second look mitigates this first impression. Quite a few ecological labels exist (SmartWood, Scientific Certification Systems, Certified Wood Products Council, Good Wood, Forest Stewardship Council), which may create confusion and decrease the clarity of the boycott. Consumers might be lost in determining which label is the most environmentally friendly, which creates an indirect cost of information searching (decreasing T^c).

Moreover, boycotting consumers are mainly in developed countries, while the most important part of tropical timber is consumed in the country of production (low α, increasing T^f). The World Resource Institute estimates that only 20 percent of the wood produced is exported (Rezende de

Azevedo *et al.* 2001). The potential impact of the boycotting population is thus fairly small, because tropical timber offers multiple markets options, which reduces the influence of the boycott.

Overall, the boycott of non-certified timber, although presenting a small opportunity cost, does not offer much potential for success, mainly because the population affected is too small.

6.5 Conclusion

This chapter explores the causes of ineffectiveness of consumer boycotts. First, consumer boycotts are affected by the usual problems of collective action. Indeed, the individual choice of boycotting has a marginal impact on the chance of success, creating a voter's paradox mechanism enhancing free-riding behaviors. Moreover, the lack of coordination may be a major source of ineffectiveness.

Second, market structure is a crucial determinant of the boycott's success. Competition increases the probability of the clean technology being present on the market. Indeed, if there is free entry, there is room for ecological certification and green labeling: a firm may choose to enter the market and to produce the good with the clean technology, if it is profitable. In that case, there is a perfect substitute on the market. In a monopoly case, consumer boycotts are less likely to succeed, because there is no good substitute for which the environmentalists can switch their consumption.

On the demand side, consumer boycotts unsurprisingly require large concerned population to be effective. More provocatively, environmental preferences have an ambiguous effect on the potential for success. Indeed, while strong environmental preferences imply smaller cost of boycotting, they also involve a weaker hurting capacity on the part of boycotting consumers. This might explain why there are so few successful boycotts in real life: boycotting groups are usually composed of consumers with small boycotting costs, whose boycott does not hurt the targeted firm's profit enough to make it change its behavior.

A potentially effective policy for NGOs would thus be to work on the proportion of the population sensitive to the quality of the environment. Indeed, the game presented here is static, but it is informative, and educating consumers may increase their awareness of environmental degradation, especially the degradation for which they are responsible. The objective of this policy would have two main consequences in the long run. First, it would induce a decrease in overall consumption, which would reduce environmental degradation. Second, it would increase the population likely to participate in environmental boycotts. In the long run, the combination of education and boycotts would increase the potential for environmental friendly technology adoption.

Appendix 6A: Basics of consumer theory

UTILITY OF THE DIRTY TECHNOLOGY

Suppose that consumers both care about their levels of consumption x and the pollution involved in consumption ex, $U_1 = U(x, ex)$, with standard assumptions $U_x > 0$, $U_{xx} < 0$, $U_e < 0$, and $U_{ee} < 0$ (subscripts denote derivatives).

ENVIRONMENTAL PREFERENCES AND LEVELS OF CONSUMPTION

Consider two consumers s and w with different environmental preferences, such that $-U_e^s > -U_e^w$, $\forall e > 0$. s thus has stronger environmental preferences (larger disutility from pollution) than w. When choosing their optimal levels of consumption, and following basic consumer theory, first-order conditions of the utility function thus yield $U_x^s + U_e^s e = U_x^w + U_e^w e$. It is straightforward that $U_x^s > U_x^w$. Given the concavity of the utility function with respect to consumption, consumers with stronger environmental preferences have lower levels of polluting consumption than others: $x^s < x^w$.

FIRM'S PROFIT WHEN BOYCOTTED

When the firm is boycotted, its profit falls: $\pi_1 > \lambda\gamma\pi_1$. γ unambiguously depends on the quantities previously consumed by boycotting consumers. Considering the previous proposition, consumer boycotts are less costly to the targeted firm when boycotting consumers have strong environmental preferences.

Appendix 6B: Factors influencing T^f

Note that ρ is likely to be smaller than 1, thus $\frac{1}{\ln\rho} < 0$.

$$\frac{\partial T^f}{\partial \pi_2} = \frac{1}{(\pi_2 - \lambda\gamma\pi_1)\ln\rho} < 0$$

$$\frac{\partial T^f}{\partial \pi_1} = \frac{-1}{(1 - \lambda\gamma)\pi_1 \ln\rho} > 0$$

$$\frac{\partial T^f}{\partial \gamma} = \frac{\lambda(\pi_2 - \pi_1)}{(\pi_2 - \lambda\gamma\pi_1)(1 - \lambda\gamma)\ln\rho} > 0$$

$$\frac{\partial T^f}{\partial \lambda} = \frac{\gamma(\pi_2 - \pi_1)}{(\pi_2 - \lambda\gamma\pi_1)(1 - \lambda\gamma)\ln\rho} > 0$$

Appendix 6C: Factors influencing T^c

$$\frac{\partial T^c}{\partial U1} = \frac{1}{(U_1 - U_b)\ln\rho} < 0$$

$$\frac{\partial T^c}{\partial U2} = \frac{-1}{(U_2 - U_b)\ln\rho} > 0$$

$$\frac{\partial T^c}{\partial U_b} = \frac{U_1 - U_2}{(U_1 - U_b)(U_2 - U_b)\ln\rho} > 0$$

References

Baron, D. (2002) Private politics and private policy: A theory of boycotts. Research Paper No. 1766, Stanford University.

Burton, P. (2004) Hugging trees: Claiming de facto property rights by blockading resource use. *Environmental and Resource Economics*, 27: 135–63.

Davidson, D. K. (1995) Ten tips for boycott targets. *Business Horizons*, 38(2): 77–80.

Diermeier, D. and Van Mieghem, J. (2005) A stochastic model of consumer boycotts. Department of Managerial Economics and Decision Sciences (MEDS), Kellogg School of Management, Northwestern University.

Friedman, M. (1985) Consumer boycotts in the United States, 1970–1980. *Journal of Consumer Affairs*, 19: 98–117.

Friedman, M. (1991) Consumer boycotts: A conceptual framework and research agenda. *Journal of Social Issues*, 47: 149–68.

Friedman, M. (1995) American consumer boycotts in response to rising food prices: Housewives' protests at the grassroots level. *Journal of Consumer Policy*, 18: 55–72.

Friedman, M. (1999) *Consumer Boycotts: Effecting Change through the Marketplace and the Media*. New York: Routledge.

Fudenberg, D. and Tirole, J. (1991) *Game Theory*. Cambridge, MA: MIT Press.

Garrett, D. E. (1987) The effectiveness of marketing policy boycotts: Environmental opposition to marketing. *Journal of Marketing*, 51(2): 46–57.

Granovetter, M. (1978) Threshold models of collective behavior. *American Journal of Sociology*, 83(6): 1420.

Innes, R. (2006) A theory of consumer boycotts under symmetric information and imperfect competition. *Economic Journal*, 116: 355–81.

Klooster, D. (2005) Environmental certification of forests: The evolution of environmental governance in a commodity network. *Journal of Rural Studies*, 21(4): 403–17.

Koku, P., Akighbe, A. and Springer, T. (1997) The financial impact of boycotts and threats of boycott. *Journal of Business Research*, 40: 15–20.

Pruitt, S. and Friedman, M. (1986) Determining the effectiveness of consumer boycotts: A stock price analysis and their impact on corporate targets. *Journal of Consumer Policy*, 9: 375–87.

Rezende de Azevedo, T., Giacini de Freitas, A. and Donovan, R. D. (2001) Forest certification – a catalyst of forest conservation? http://www.rainforest-alliance.org/forestry/documents/catalyst.pdf

Skjærseth, J. B. and Skodvin, T. (2001) Climate change and the oil industry: Common problems, different strategies. *Global Environmental Politics*, 1(4): 43–64.

Smith, N. (1990) *Morality and the Market. Consumer Pressure for Corporate Accountability*. London: Routledge.

Teoh, S., Welch, I. and Wazzan, C. (1999) The effect of socially activist investment policies on the financial markets: Evidence from the South African boycott. *Journal of Business*, 72: 35–89.

Tyran, J. and Engelmann, D. (2005) To buy or not to buy? An experimental study of consumer boycotts in retail markets. *Economica*, 72: 1–16.

Zyglidopoulos, S. (2002) The social and environmental responsibilities of multinationals: Evidence from the Brent Spar case. *Journal of Business Ethics*, 36(1–2): 141–51.

Notes

1 Agricultural expansion, forest products as safety nets and deforestation

1 The term "non-timber forest product" encompasses all biological materials other than timber which are extracted from forests for human use.
2 For an analysis of the interactions between labor market and deforestation, see Bluffstone (1995).

2 Commons as insurance: safety nets or poverty traps?

1 Note here that the size of the CPR is fixed, and therefore not a choice variable. Chapter 1 above considers the impact of NTFP extraction as insurance on deforestation.
2 Assuming common knowledge on outcome realizations and no principal-agent related issues.

3 How size of concessions may influence systemic corruption in forest harvesting: a theoretical assessment

1 For an overview of corruption and illegal activities in the forestry sector, see Contreras-Hermosilla (2001) and Callister (1999).
2 The case of an environmental tax is addressed in Wilson and Damania (2005). The level of non-compliance would then reduce the tax basis.
3 Equivalently, we can assume that every firm is audited, and that σ represents the probability of detection by the authority.
4 The subscripts refer to first and second derivatives.

4 Unsustainable timber harvesting, deforestation and the role of certification

1 Corruption, which can be considered as a better proxy in this context, will be considered in the cross-section analysis to check the robustness of our analysis.
2 We also tested the impact (i) of the real effective exchange rate on deforestation, as in Arcand *et al.* (2008); (ii) of cross-boundary effects by introducing exports of forest products ($Export$; source: WRI; expected sign +). Indeed, unsustainable harvest may be driven by the growing demand for timber products in emerging countries like India or China. However, we could not find evidence of such relationships, and then dropped those two variables from our regressions.

3 We check the robustness of this assumption by performing a Hausman test. In all models we estimated, we can reject the null hypothesis that the coefficients estimated by random-effects estimator are the same as those estimated by the fixed-effects estimator. Fixed effects are thus appropriate here.

4 Drukker (2003) displays simulation results to show the good size and power properties of the test with good sized samples.

5 First difference (FD) estimators are more efficient than FE if u_{it} follows a random walk. Indeed, both estimators are unbiased and consistent with T fixed as $N \to \infty$, but FD corrects for first-order autocorrelation, i.e. if the deforestation process exhibits some substantial and positive correlation. Since, in contrast with Scrieciu (2007), we do not find evidence of such an issue with our database, then FE is appropriate.

6 In addition, adding time dummies is likely to remove any potential presence of heteroskedasticity (Roodman 2009).

7 That is, $\sigma(i)^2 = \sigma^2$ for all i.

8 As a robustness check, the presence of heteroskedasticity has also been corrected by normalizing roundwood production to GDP. Similar results are found (available upon request).

9 Our model has low explanatory power for our set of developed countries ($R^2 = 5$ percent). Nevertheless, the *Harvest-volume* variable was significant at 15 percent for both the FE and double FE models. *Harvest-value* is significant at 15 percent and 1 percent for the FE and double FE models, respectively. Results are available upon request.

10 An other alternative approach (e.g. Hsiao 1986) is to first estimate a fixed-effect model and then run a second regression in which the coefficients on the country fixed effects from the first regression become the dependent variable and explanatory variables are time-invariant variables such as the initial forest cover. The coefficients values need to be interpreted cautiously, however.

11 The board of FSC International consists of three chambers: economic, social and environment. The code of conduct that has been decided is composed of 10 principles that define the certification criteria (Fischer *et al.* 2005).

12 Other institution proxies were available in the cross-section analysis, which could fit better with the issue of deforestation. Nevertheless, we chose to keep the Freedom House index in order to get a database consistent with the previous section. However, the use of a corruption perception index (WRI) and of a rule of law index (Kaufman *et al.* 2008) as proxies for institutional quality turned out to provide similar results.

13 The addition of other possible determinants of deforestation (*Exports* of forest products in 2005, for instance) does not change the significance of our findings. Moreover, testing our model with arable cropland as a deforestation proxy leads to similar results. Finally, our coefficients of interest are quite stable.

6 On the sources of consumer boycotts ineffectiveness

1 Consumers are classified according to their environmental preferences: consumer 1 has the highest environmental preferences and individual N has the lowest environmental preferences.

2 The formation of beliefs is not considered here. This belief structure may be due to the firm's reputation or past boycott experiences.

3 War of attrition models are well documented in the economics literature. See Fudenberg and Tirole (1991).
4 We assume that the firm can only use one technology. Thus, it cannot diversify its production process, producing the good with both technologies at the same time.

Index